Real-World Software Development
A Project-Driven Guide to Fundamentals in Java

Raoul-Gabriel Urma and Richard Warburton

Beijing · Boston · Farnham · Sebastopol · Tokyo

Real-World Software Development

by Raoul-Gabriel Urma and Richard Warburton

Published by O'Reilly Media, Inc., 1005 Gravenstein Highway North, Sebastopol, CA 95472.

O'Reilly books may be purchased for educational, business, or sales promotional use. Online editions are also available for most titles (*http://oreilly.com*). For more information, contact our corporate/institutional sales department: 800-998-9938 or *corporate@oreilly.com*.

Editor: Alicia Young	**Indexer:** Ellen Troutman-Zaig
Production Editor: Kristen Brown	**Interior Designer:** David Futato
Copyeditor: Kim Cofer	**Cover Designer:** Karen Montgomery
Proofreader: Tracy Brown-Hamilton	**Illustrator:** Rebecca Demarest

December 2019:   First Edition

Revision History for the First Edition
2019-12-02:   First Release

See *http://oreilly.com/catalog/errata.csp?isbn=9781491967171* for release details.

978-1-491-96717-1

[LSI]

Table of Contents

Preface

Mastering software development involves learning a disparate set of concepts. If you're starting out as a junior software developer, or even if you're more experienced, it can seem like an insurmountable hurdle. Should you be spending time learning about established topics in the object-oriented world such as SOLID principles, design patterns, or test-driven development? Should you be trying out things that are becoming increasingly popular such as functional programming?

Even once you've picked some topics to learn it's often hard to identify how they fit together. When you should go down the route of applying functional programming ideas in your project? When do you worry about testing? How do you know at what point to introduce or refine these techniques? Do you need to read a book on each of these topics and then another set of blog posts or videos to explain how to put things together? Where do you even start?

Don't worry, this book is here to help you. You will be helped through an integrated, project-driven approach to learning. You'll learn the core topics that you need to know in order to become a productive developer. Not only that, but we show how these things fit together into bigger projects.

Why We Wrote This Book

Over the years we have built up a wealth of experience around teaching developers to code. We have both written books on Java 8 onward and run training courses around professional software development. In the process we've been recognized as Java Champions and international conference speakers.

We've found over the years that many developers could benefit from either an introduction or a refresher on several core topics. Design patterns, functional programming, SOLID principles, and testing are practices that often get good coverage in their own right, but it's rarely shown how they work well and fit together. People sometimes even get put off from improving their skills simply due to the paralysis of choice over what to learn. We want to not only teach people core skills, but do so in a way that's easy to approach and fun, too.

A Developer-Oriented Approach

This book also gives you the opportunity to learn in a developer-oriented way. It contains plenty of code samples and whenever we introduce a topic we always provide concrete code examples. You get all the code for the projects within the book, so if you want to follow along you can even step through the book code in an *Integrated Development Environment* (IDE) or run the programs in order to try them out.

Another common bugbear when it comes to technical books is that they are often written in a formal, lecturing style. That's not how normal people speak to each other! In this book you'll get a conversational style that helps to engage you in the content rather than being patronizing.

What's in the Book?

Each chapter is structured around a software project. At the end of a chapter, if you've been following along, you should be able to write that project. The projects start off as simple command-line batch programs but grow in complexity to fully fledged applications.

You'll benefit from a project-driven structure in a variety of ways. First, you get to see how different programming techniques work together in an integrated setting. When we look at functional programming toward the end of the book, it isn't just abstract collection-processing operations—they're presented in order to calculate actual results used by the project in question. This solves the problem of educational material showing good ideas or approaches, but developers often use them inappropriately or out of context.

Second, a project-driven approach helps ensure that at each stage you see realistic examples. Educational materials are often full of example classes called Foo and methods called bar. Our examples are relevant to the projects in question and show how to apply the ideas to real problems, similar to the ones that you may encounter in your career.

Finally, it's more fun and engaging to learn this way. Each chapter is a fresh project and a fresh opportunity to learn new things. We want you to read through to the end and really enjoy turning the pages as you're reading. The chapters start with a challenge that will be solved, walk you through the solution, and then end by evaluating what you learned and how the challenge was solved. We specifically call out the challenge at the beginning and end of every chapter to ensure that its goals are clear to you.

Who Should Read This Book?

We're confident that developers from a wide variety of backgrounds will find things that are useful and interesting in this book. Having said that, there are some people who will get the maximum value out of this book.

Junior software developers, often just out of university or a couple of years into their programming career, are who we think of as the core audience for this book. You'll learn about fundamental topics that we expect to be of relevance throughout your software development career. You don't need to have a university degree by any means, but you do need to know the basics of programming in order to make the best use of this book. We won't explain what an if statement or a loop is, for example.

You don't need to know much about object-oriented or functional programming in order to get started. In Chapter 2, we make no assumptions beyond that you know what a class is and can use collections with generics (e.g., List<String>). We take it right from the basics.

Another group who will find this book of particular interest is developers learning Java while coming from another programming language, such as C#, C++, or Python. This book helps you quickly get up to speed with the language constructs and also the principles, practices, and idioms that are important to write good Java code.

If you're a more experienced Java developer, you may want to skip Chapter 2 in order to avoid repeating basic material that you already know, but Chapter 3 onward will be full of concepts and approaches that will be of benefit to many developers.

We've found that learning can be one of the most fun parts of software development and hope that you'll find that as well when reading this book. We hope you have fun on this journey.

Conventions Used in This Book

The following typographical conventions are used in this book:

Italic
: Indicates new terms, URLs, email addresses, filenames, and file extensions.

`Constant width`
: Used for program listings, as well as within paragraphs to refer to program elements such as variable or function names, databases, data types, environment variables, statements, and keywords.

`Constant width bold`
: Shows commands or other text that should be typed literally by the user.

`Constant width italic`

Shows text that should be replaced with user-supplied values or by values determined by context.

 This element signifies a general note.

Using Code Examples

Supplemental material (code examples, exercises, etc.) is available for download at *https://github.com/Iteratr-Learning/Real-World-Software-Development*.

If you have a technical question or a problem using the code examples, please send email to *bookquestions@oreilly.com*.

This book is here to help you get your job done. In general, if example code is offered with this book, you may use it in your programs and documentation. You do not need to contact us for permission unless you're reproducing a significant portion of the code. For example, writing a program that uses several chunks of code from this book does not require permission. Selling or distributing examples from O'Reilly books does require permission. Answering a question by citing this book and quoting example code does not require permission. Incorporating a significant amount of example code from this book into your product's documentation does require permission.

We appreciate, but generally do not require, attribution. An attribution usually includes the title, author, publisher, and ISBN. For example: "*Real-World Software Development* by Raoul-Gabriel Urma and Richard Warburton (O'Reilly). Copyright 2020 Functor Ltd. and Monotonic Ltd., 978-1-491-96717-1."

If you feel your use of code examples falls outside fair use or the permission given above, feel free to contact us at *permissions@oreilly.com*.

O'Reilly Online Learning

 For more than 40 years, *O'Reilly Media* has provided technology and business training, knowledge, and insight to help companies succeed.

Our unique network of experts and innovators share their knowledge and expertise through books, articles, conferences, and our online learning platform. O'Reilly's online learning platform gives you on-demand access to live training courses, in-depth learning paths, interactive coding environments, and a vast collection of text and video from O'Reilly and 200+ other publishers. For more information, please visit *http://oreilly.com*.

How to Contact Us

Please address comments and questions concerning this book to the publisher:

O'Reilly Media, Inc.
1005 Gravenstein Highway North
Sebastopol, CA 95472
800-998-9938 (in the United States or Canada)
707-829-0515 (international or local)
707-829-0104 (fax)

We have a web page for this book, where we list errata, examples, and any additional information. You can access this page at *https://oreil.ly/RealWorld_SoftwareDev*.

Email *bookquestions@oreilly.com* to comment or ask technical questions about this book.

For more information about our books, courses, conferences, and news, see our website at *http://www.oreilly.com*.

Find us on Facebook: *http://facebook.com/oreilly*

Follow us on Twitter: *http://twitter.com/oreillymedia*

Watch us on YouTube: *http://www.youtube.com/oreillymedia*

CHAPTER 1

Starting the Journey

In this chapter, we'll give you an introduction to the concepts and principles of this book. A good way of summarizing the overall approach is *Practices and Principles over Technology*. There are already many books about specific technologies, and we aren't seeking to add to that enormous pile. That isn't to say that the detailed knowledge that is specific to a given language, framework, or library isn't useful. It's just that it has a shorter shelf-life than general practices and principles that apply over longer periods of time and across different languages and frameworks. That's where this book can help you.

Themes

Throughout the book we've used a project-based structure to aid learning. It's worth thinking about the different themes that run through the chapters, how they link up together, and why we chose them. Following are the four different themes that weave through the chapters.

Java Features

Structuring code with classes and interfaces is discussed in Chapter 2. We move onto exceptions and packages in Chapter 3. You will also get a short overview of lambda expressions in Chapter 3. Then local variable type inferences and switch expressions are explained in Chapter 5, and finally lambda expressions and method references are covered in detail in Chapter 7. Java language features are important because so many software projects are written in Java, so it's useful language to know the workings of it. Many of these language features are useful in other programming languages as well, such as C#, C++, Ruby, or Python. Even though those languages have differences, understanding the how to use a class and core OOP concepts will be valuable across different languages.

Software Design and Architecture

Throughout the book a series of design patterns are introduced that help provide you with common solutions to common problems that developers encounter. These are important to know because even though it may seem like every software project is different and comes with its own set of problems, in practice many of these have been encountered before. Understanding common problems and solutions that have been solved by developers keeps you from reinventing the wheel in a new software project and enables you to deliver software faster and more reliably.

The higher-level concepts of coupling and cohesion are introduced early on the book in Chapter 2. The Notification pattern is introduced in Chapter 3. How to design a user-friendly Fluent API and the Builder pattern are introduced in Chapter 5. We look at the big-picture concepts of event-driven and hexagonal architectures in Chapter 6 and the Repository pattern in Chapter 7. Finally, you're also introduced to functional programming in Chapter 7.

SOLID

We cover all the SOLID principles throughout various chapters. These are a set of principles designed to help make software easier to maintain. While we like to think of writing software as the fun part, if the software that you write is successful it will need to evolve, grow, and be maintained. Trying to make the software as easy to maintain as possible helps this evolution, maintenance, and long-term addition of features. The SOLID principles and the chapters where we will discuss them are:

- Single Responsibility Principle (SRP), discussed in Chapter 2
- Open/Closed Principle (OCP), discussed in Chapter 3
- Liskov Substitution Principle (LSP), discussed in Chapter 4
- Interface Segregation Principle (ISP), discussed in Chapter 5
- Dependency Inversion Principle (DIP), discussed in Chapter 7

Testing

Writing reliable code that can be easily evolved over time is really important. Automated tests are key to this. As the software that you write scales in size it becomes increasingly hard to manually test different possible cases. You need to automate your testing processes to avoid the days of human effort it would take to test your software without it.

You learn about the basics of writing tests in Chapters 2 and 4. This is extended to test-driven development, or TDD, in Chapter 5. In Chapter 6 we cover the use of test doubles, including mocks and stubs.

Chapter Summary

Here's the outline of the chapters.

Chapter 2, The Bank Statements Analyzer
> You'll write a program to analyze bank statements in order to help people understand their finances better. This will help you to learn more about core object-oriented design techniques such as *Single Responsibility Principle* (SRP), coupling, and cohesion.

Chapter 3, Extending the Bank Statements Analyzer
> In this chapter you learn how to extend the code from Chapter 2, adding more features, using the Strategy Design pattern, the Open/Closed Principle, and how to model failures using exceptions.

Chapter 4, The Document Management System
> In this chapter we help a successful doctor manage her patient records better. This introduces concepts such as inheritance within software design, the Liskov Substitution Principle, and tradeoffs between composition and inheritance. You will also learn how to write more reliable software with automated test code.

Chapter 5, The Business Rules Engine
> You'll learn about building a core business rules engine—a way of defining business logic that is flexible and easy to maintain. This chapter introduces the topics of test-driven development, developing a Fluent API, and the Interface Segregation Principle.

Chapter 6, Twootr
> *Twootr* is a messaging platform that enables people to broadcast short messages to other users who follow them. This chapter builds out the core of a simple Twootr system. You'll learn how to think outside-in—to go from requirements through to the core of your application. You'll also learn how to use test doubles to isolate and test interactions from different components within your codebase.

Chapter 7, Extending Twootr
> The final project-based chapter in the book extends the Twootr implementation from the previous chapter. It explains the Dependency Inversion Principle and introduces bigger picture architectural choices such as event-driven and hexagonal architectures. This chapter can help you extend your knowledge of automated testing by covering test doubles, such as stubs and mocks, and also functional programming techniques.

Chapter 8, Conclusion
> This final concluding chapter revisits the major themes and concepts of the book and offers additional resources as you continue in your programming career.

Iterating on You

As a software developer you may well approach projects in an iterative fashion. That's to say, slice off the highest priority week or two's worth of work items, implement them, and then use the feedback in order to decide on the next set of items. We've found that it's often worth evaluating the progress of your own skills in the same way.

At the end of every chapter there is a brief "Iterating on You" section with a few suggestions on how you improve upon on the learning from the chapter in your own time.

Now that you know what you can expect from this book, let's get to work!

CHAPTER 2

The Bank Statements Analyzer

The Challenge

The FinTech industry is really hot right now. Mark Erbergzuck realizes that he spends a lot of money on different purchases and would benefit from automatically summarizing his expenses. He receives monthly statements from his bank, but he finds them a bit overwhelming. He has tasked you with developing a piece of software that will automate the processing of his bank statements so he can get better insights into his finances. Challenge accepted!

The Goal

In this chapter, you will learn the foundations about good software development before learning more advanced techniques in the next few chapters.

You will start off by implementing the problem statement in one single class. You will then explore why this approach poses several challenges in terms of coping for changing requirements and maintenance of the project.

But do not worry! You will learn software design principles and techniques to adopt to ensure that the code you write meets these criteria. You will first learn about the *Single Responsibility Principle* (SRP), which helps develop software that is more maintainable, easier to comprehend, and reduces the scope for introducing new bugs. Along the way, you will pick up new concepts such as *cohesion* and *coupling*, which are useful characteristics to guide you about the quality of the code and software that you develop.

This chapter uses libraries and features from Java 8 and above, including the new date and time library.

If at any point you want to look at the source code for this chapter, you can look at the package `com.iteratrlearning.shu_book.chapter_02` in the book's code repository.

Bank Statements Analyzer Requirements

You had a delicious hipster latte (no added sugar) with Mark Erbergzuck to gather requirements. Because Mark is pretty tech-savvy, he tells you that the bank statements analyzer just needs to read a text file containing a list of bank transactions. He downloads the file from his online banking portal. This text is structured using a comma-separated values (CSV) format. Here is a sample of bank transactions:

```
30-01-2017,-100,Deliveroo
30-01-2017,-50,Tesco
01-02-2017,6000,Salary
02-02-2017,2000,Royalties
02-02-2017,-4000,Rent
03-02-2017,3000,Tesco
05-02-2017,-30,Cinema
```

He would like to get an answer for the following queries:

- What is the total profit and loss from a list of bank statements? Is it positive or negative?
- How many bank transactions are there in a particular month?
- What are his top-10 expenses?
- Which category does he spend most of his money on?

KISS Principle

Let's start simple. How about the first query: "What is the total profit and loss from a list of bank statements?" You need to process a CSV file and calculate the sum of all the amounts. Since there is nothing else required, you may decide that there is no need to create a very complex application.

You can "Keep It Short and Simple" (KISS) and have the application code in one single class as shown in Example 2-1. Note that you do not have to worry about possible exceptions yet (e.g., what if the file does not exist or what if parsing a loaded file fails?). That is a topic that you will learn about in Chapter 3.

CSV is not fully standardized. It's often referred to as values separated by commas. However, some people refer to it as a delimiter-separated format that uses different delimiters, such as semicolons or tabs. These requirements can add more complexity to the implementation of a parser. In this chapter, we will assume that values are separated by a comma (,).

Example 2-1. Calculating the sum of all statements

```java
public class BankTransactionAnalyzerSimple {
    private static final String RESOURCES = "src/main/resources/";

    public static void main(final String... args) throws IOException {

        final Path path = Paths.get(RESOURCES + args[0]);
        final List<String> lines = Files.readAllLines(path);
        double total = 0d;
        for(final String line: lines) {
            final String[] columns = line.split(",");
            final double amount = Double.parseDouble(columns[1]);
            total += amount;
        }

        System.out.println("The total for all transactions is " + total);
    }
}
```

What is happening here? You are loading the CSV file passed as a command-line argument to the application. The `Path` class represents a path in the filesystem. You then use `Files.readAllLines()` to return a list of lines. Once you have all the lines from the file, you can parse them one at a time by:

- Splitting the columns by commas
- Extracting the amount
- Parsing the amount to a `double`

Once you have the amount for a given statement as a `double` you can then add it to the current total. At the end of the processing, you will have the total amount.

The code in Example 2-1 will work fine, but it misses a few corner cases that are always good to think about when writing production-ready code:

- What if the file is empty?
- What if parsing the amount fails because the data was corrupted?
- What if a statement line has missing data?

We will come back to the topic of dealing with exceptions in Chapter 3, but it is a good habit to keep these types of questions in mind.

How about solving the second query: "How many bank transactions are there in a particular month?" What can you do? Copy and paste is a simple technique, right? You could just copy and paste the same code and replace the logic so it selects the given month, as shown in Example 2-2.

Example 2-2. Calculating the sum of January statements

```
final Path path = Paths.get(RESOURCES + args[0]);
final List<String> lines = Files.readAllLines(path);
double total = 0d;
final DateTimeFormatter DATE_PATTERN = DateTimeFormatter.ofPattern("dd-MM-yyyy");
for(final String line: lines) {
    final String[] columns = line.split(",");
    final LocalDate date = LocalDate.parse(columns[0], DATE_PATTERN);
    if(date.getMonth() == Month.JANUARY) {
        final double amount = Double.parseDouble(columns[1]);
        total += amount;
    }
}

System.out.println("The total for all transactions in January is " + total);
```

final Variables

As a short detour, we'll explain the use of the final keyword in the code examples. Throughout this book we've used the final keyword fairly extensively. Marking a local variable or a field final means that it cannot be re-assigned. Whether you use final or not in your project is a collective matter for your team and project since its use has both benefits and drawbacks. We've found that marking as many variables final as possible clearly demarcates what state is mutated during the lifetime of an object and what state isn't re-assigned.

On the other hand, the use of the final keyword doesn't guarantee immutability of the object in question. You can have a final field that refers to an object with mutable state. We will be discussing immutability in more detail in Chapter 4. Furthermore, its use also adds a lot of boilerplate to the codebase. Some teams pick the compromise position of having final fields on method parameters, in order to ensure that they are clearly not re-assigned and not local variables.

One area where there is little point in using the final keyword, although the Java language allows it, is for method parameters on abstract methods; for example, in interfaces. This is because the lack of body means that there is no real implication or meaning to the final keyword in this situation. Arguably the use of final has diminished since the introduction of the var keyword in Java 10, and we discuss this concept later in Example 5-15.

Code Maintainability and Anti-Patterns

Do you think the copy-and-paste approach demonstrated in Example 2-2 is a good idea? Time to take a step back and reflect on what is happening. When you write code, you should strive for providing good *code maintainability*. What does this mean? It is best described by a wish list of properties about the code you write:

- It should be simple to locate code responsible for a particular feature.
- It should be simple to understand what the code does.
- It should be simple to add or remove a new feature.
- It should provide good *encapsulation*. In other words, implementation details should be hidden from a user of your code so it is easier to understand and make changes.

A good way to think about the impact of the code you write is to consider what happens if a work colleague of yours has to look at your code in six months and you have moved to a different company.

Ultimately your goal is to manage the complexity of the application you are building. However, if you keep on copy pasting the same code as new requirements come in, you will end up with the following issues, which are called *anti-patterns* because they are common ineffective solutions:

- Hard to understand code because you have one giant *"God Class"*
- Code that is brittle and easily broken by changes because of *code duplication*

Let's explain these two anti-patterns in more detail.

God Class

By putting all of your code in one file, you end up with one giant class making it harder to understand its purpose because that class is responsible for everything! If you need to update the logic of existing code (e.g., change how the parsing works) how will you easily locate that code and make changes? This problem is referred to as the anti-pattern "God Class." Essentially you have one class that does everything. You should avoid this. In the next section, you will learn about the *Single Responsibility Principle*, which is a software development guideline to help write code that is easier to understand and maintain.

Code Duplication

For each query, you are duplicating the logic for reading and parsing the input. What if the input required is no longer CSV but a JSON file? What if multiple formats need to be supported? Adding such a feature will be a painful change because your code has hardcoded one specific solution and duplicated that behavior in multiple places. Consequently, all the places will all have to change and you will potentially introduce new bugs.

 You will often hear about the "Don't Repeat Yourself" (DRY) principle. It is the idea that when you successfully reduce repetition, a modification of the logic does not require multiple modifications of your code anymore.

A related problem is what if the data format changes? The code only supports a specific data format pattern. If it needs to be enhanced (e.g., new columns) or a different data format needs to be supported (e.g., different attribute names) you will again have to make many changes across your code.

The conclusion is that it is good to keep things simple when possible, but do not abuse the KISS principle. Instead, you need to reflect on the design of your whole application and have an understanding of how to break down the problem into separate sub-problems that are easier to manage individually. The result is that you will have code that is easier to understand, maintain, and adapt to new requirements.

Single Responsibility Principle

The *Single Responsibility Principle* (SRP) is a general software development guideline to follow that contributes to writing code that is easier to manage and maintain.

You can think about SRP in two complementary ways:

- A class has responsibility over a single functionality
- There is only one single reason for a class to change[1]

The SRP is usually applied to classes and methods. SRP is concerned with one particular behavior, concept, or category. It leads to code that is more robust because there is one specific reason why it should change rather than multiple concerns. The reason why multiple concerns is problematic is, as you saw earlier, it complicates code

---

1 This definition is attributed to Robert Martin.

maintainability by potentially introducing bugs in several places. It can also make the code harder to understand and change.

So how do you apply SRP in the code shown in Example 2-2? It is clear that the main class has multiple responsibilities that can be broken down individually:

1. Reading input

2. Parsing the input in a given format

3. Processing the result

4. Reporting a summary of the result

We will focus on the parsing part in this chapter. You will learn how to extend the Bank Statements Analyzer in the next chapter so that it is completely modularized.

The first natural step is to extract the CSV parsing logic into a separate class so you can reuse it for different processing queries. Let's call it `BankStatementCSVParser` so it is immediately clear what it does (Example 2-3).

Example 2-3. Extracting the parsing logic in a separate class

```java
public class BankStatementCSVParser {

    private static final DateTimeFormatter DATE_PATTERN
        = DateTimeFormatter.ofPattern("dd-MM-yyyy");

    private BankTransaction parseFromCSV(final String line) {
        final String[] columns = line.split(",");

        final LocalDate date = LocalDate.parse(columns[0], DATE_PATTERN);
        final double amount = Double.parseDouble(columns[1]);
        final String description = columns[2];

        return new BankTransaction(date, amount, description);
    }

    public List<BankTransaction> parseLinesFromCSV(final List<String> lines) {
        final List<BankTransaction> bankTransactions = new ArrayList<>();
        for(final String line: lines) {
            bankTransactions.add(parseFromCSV(line));
        }
        return bankTransactions;
    }
}
```

You can see that the class `BankStatementCSVParser` declares two methods, `parseFromCSV()` and `parseLinesFromCSV()`, that generate `BankTransaction` objects, which is a domain class that models a bank statement (see Example 2-4 for its declaration).

What does *domain* mean? It means the use of words and terminology that match the business problem (i.e., the domain at hand).

The BankTransaction class is useful so that different parts of our application share the same common understanding of what a bank statement is. You will notice that the class provides implementation for the methods equals and hashcode. The purpose of these methods and how to implement them correctly is covered in Chapter 6.

Example 2-4. A domain class for a bank transaction

```java
public class BankTransaction {
    private final LocalDate date;
    private final double amount;
    private final String description;


    public BankTransaction(final LocalDate date, final double amount, final String
description) {
        this.date = date;
        this.amount = amount;
        this.description = description;
    }

    public LocalDate getDate() {
        return date;
    }

    public double getAmount() {
        return amount;
    }

    public String getDescription() {
        return description;
    }

    @Override
    public String toString() {
        return "BankTransaction{" +
                "date=" + date +
                ", amount=" + amount +
                ", description='" + description + '\'' +
                '}';
    }

    @Override
    public boolean equals(Object o) {
        if (this == o) return true;
```

```
        if (o == null || getClass() != o.getClass()) return false;
        BankTransaction that = (BankTransaction) o;
        return Double.compare(that.amount, amount) == 0 &&
                date.equals(that.date) &&
                description.equals(that.description);
    }

    @Override
    public int hashCode() {
        return Objects.hash(date, amount, description);
    }
}
```

Now you can refactor the application so that it uses your BankStatementCSVParser, in particular its parseLinesFromCSV() method, as shown in Example 2-5.

Example 2-5. Using the bank statement CSV parser

```
final BankStatementCSVParser bankStatementParser = new BankTransactionCSVParser();

final String fileName = args[0];
final Path path = Paths.get(RESOURCES + fileName);
final List<String> lines = Files.readAllLines(path);

final List<BankTransaction> bankTransactions
    = bankStatementParser.parseLinesFromCSV(lines);

System.out.println("The total for all transactions is " + calculateTotalAmount(bank
Transactions));
System.out.println("Transactions in January " + selectInMonth(BankTransactions,
Month.JANUARY));
```

The different queries you have to implement no longer need to know about internal parsing details, as you can now use BankTransaction objects directly to extract the information required. The code in Example 2-6 shows how to declare the methods calculateTotalAmount() and selectInMonth(), which are responsible for processing the list of transactions and returning an appropriate result. In Chapter 3 you will get an overview of lambda expressions and the Streams API, which will help tidy the code further.

Example 2-6. Processing lists of bank transactions

```
public static double calculateTotalAmount(final List<BankTransaction> bankTransac
tions) {
    double total = 0d;
    for(final BankTransaction bankTransaction: bankTransactions) {
        total += bankTransaction.getAmount();
    }
    return total;
```

```
    }

    public static List<BankTransaction> selectInMonth(final List<BankTransaction> bank
    Transactions, final Month month) {

        final List<BankTransaction> bankTransactionsInMonth = new ArrayList<>();
        for(final BankTransaction bankTransaction: bankTransactions) {
            if(bankTransaction.getDate().getMonth() == month) {
                bankTransactionsInMonth.add(bankTransaction);
            }
        }
        return bankTransactionsInMonth;
    }
```

The key benefit with this refactoring is that your main application is no longer responsible for the implementation of the parsing logic. It is now delegating that responsibility to a separate class and methods that can be maintained and updated independently. As new requirements come in for different queries, you can reuse the functionality encapsulated by the BankStatementCSVParser class.

In addition, if you need to change the way the parsing algorithm works (e.g., a more efficient implementation that caches results), you now have just a single place that needs to change. Moreover, you introduced a class called BankTransaction that other parts of your code can rely on without depending on a specific data format pattern.

It is a good habit to follow the *principle of least surprise* when you implement methods. It will help ensure that it is obvious what is happening when looking at the code. This means:

- Use self-documenting method names so it is immediately obvious what they do (e.g., calculateTotalAmount())
- Do not change the state of parameters as other parts of code may depend on it

The principle of least surprise can be a subjective concept, though. When in doubt, speak to your colleagues and team members to ensure everyone is aligned.

Cohesion

So far you have learned about three principles: *KISS*, *DRY*, and *SRP*. But you have not learned about characteristics to reason about the quality of your code. In software engineering you will often hear about *cohesion* as an important characteristic of different parts of the code you write. It sounds fancy, but it is a really useful concept to give you an indication about the maintainability of your code.

Cohesion is concerned with *how related* things are. To be more precise, cohesion measures how strongly related responsibilities of a class or method are. In other words, how much do things belong together? It is a way to help you reason about the complexity of your software. What you want to achieve is *high cohesion*, which means that the code is easier for others to locate, understand, and use. In the code that you refactored earlier, the class `BankTransactionCSVParser` is highly cohesive. In fact, it groups together two methods that are related to parsing CSV data.

Generally, the concept of cohesion is applied to classes (class-level cohesion), but it can also be applied to methods (method-level cohesion).

If you take the entry point to your program, the class `BankStatementAnalyzer`, you will notice that its responsibility is to wire up the different parts of your application such as the parser and the calculations and report back on the screen. However, the logic responsible for doing calculations is currently declared as static methods within the `BankStatementAnalyzer`. This is an example of poor cohesion because the concerns of calculations declared in this class are not directly related to parsing or reporting.

Instead, you can extract the calculation operations into a separate class called `BankStatementProcessor`. You can also see that the list of transactions method argument is shared for all these operations, so you can include it as a field to the class. As a result, your method signatures become simpler to reason about and the class `BankStatementProcessor` is more cohesive. The code in Example 2-7 shows the end result. The additional advantage is that the methods of `BankStatementProcessor` can be reused by other parts of your application without depending on the whole `BankStatementAnalyzer`.

Example 2-7. Grouping the calculation operations in the class BankStatementProcessor

```
public class BankStatementProcessor {

    private final List<BankTransaction> bankTransactions;

    public BankStatementProcessor(final List<BankTransaction> bankTransactions) {
        this.bankTransactions = bankTransactions;
    }

    public double calculateTotalAmount() {
        double total = 0;
        for(final BankTransaction bankTransaction: bankTransactions) {
            total += bankTransaction.getAmount();
        }
        return total;
    }

    public double calculateTotalInMonth(final Month month) {
        double total = 0;
        for(final BankTransaction bankTransaction: bankTransactions) {
            if(bankTransaction.getDate().getMonth() == month) {
```

```
                    total += bankTransaction.getAmount();
            }
        }
        return total;
    }

    public double calculateTotalForCategory(final String category) {
        double total = 0;
        for(final BankTransaction bankTransaction: bankTransactions) {
            if(bankTransaction.getDescription().equals(category)) {
                total += bankTransaction.getAmount();
            }
        }
        return total;
    }
}
```

You can now make use the methods of this class with the `BankStatementAnalyzer` as shown in Example 2-8.

Example 2-8. Processing lists of bank transactions using the BankStatementProcessor class

```
public class BankStatementAnalyzer {
    private static final String RESOURCES = "src/main/resources/";
    private static final BankStatementCSVParser bankStatementParser = new BankState
mentCSVParser();

    public static void main(final String... args) throws IOException {

        final String fileName = args[0];
        final Path path = Paths.get(RESOURCES + fileName);
        final List<String> lines = Files.readAllLines(path);

        final List<BankTransaction> bankTransactions = bankStatementParser.parseLi
nesFrom(lines);
        final BankStatementProcessor bankStatementProcessor = new BankStatementPro
cessor(bankTransactions);

        collectSummary(bankStatementProcessor);
    }

    private static void collectSummary(final BankStatementProcessor bankStatementPro
cessor) {
        System.out.println("The total for all transactions is "
                + bankStatementProcessor.calculateTotalAmount());

        System.out.println("The total for transactions in January is "
                + bankStatementProcessor.calculateTotalInMonth(Month.JANUARY));

        System.out.println("The total for transactions in February is "
```

```
        + bankStatementProcessor.calculateTotalInMonth(Month.FEBRUARY));

    System.out.println("The total salary received is "
        + bankStatementProcessor.calculateTotalForCategory("Salary"));
    }
}
```

In the next subsections, you will focus on learning guidelines to help you write code that is easier to reason and maintain.

Class-Level Cohesion

In practice, you will come across at least six common ways to group methods:

- Functional
- Informational
- Utility
- Logical
- Sequential
- Temporal

Keep in mind that if the methods you are grouping are weakly related, you have low cohesion. We discuss them in order and Table 2-1 provides a summary.

Functional

The approach you took when writing the BankStatementCSVParser was to group the methods functionally. The methods parseFrom() and parseLinesFrom() are solving a defined task: parse the lines in the CSV format. In fact, the method parseLines From() uses the method parseFrom(). This is generally a good way to achieve high cohesion because the methods are working together, so it makes sense to group them so they are easier to locate and understand. The danger with functional cohesion is that it may be tempting to have a profusion of overly simplistic classes grouping only a single method. Going down the road of overly simplistic classes adds unnecessary verbosity and complexity because there are many more classes to think about.

Informational

Another reason to group methods is because they work on the same data or domain object. Say you needed a way to create, read, update, and delete BankTransaction objects (CRUD operations); you may wish to have a class dedicated for these operations. The code in Example 2-9 shows a class that exhibits informational cohesion with four different methods. Each method throws a UnsupportedOperationExcep tion to indicate the body is currently unimplemented for the purpose of the example.

Example 2-9. An example of informational cohesion

```java
public class BankTransactionDAO {

    public BankTransaction create(final LocalDate date, final double amount, final
String description) {
        // ...
        throw new UnsupportedOperationException();
    }

    public BankTransaction read(final long id) {
        // ...
        throw new UnsupportedOperationException();
    }

    public BankTransaction update(final long id) {
        // ...
        throw new UnsupportedOperationException();
    }

    public void delete(final BankTransaction BankTransaction) {
        // ...
        throw new UnsupportedOperationException();
    }
}
```

 This is a typical pattern that you see often when interfacing with a database that maintains a table for a specific domain object. This pattern is usually called *Data Access Object* (DAO) and requires some kind of ID to identify the objects. DAOs essentially abstract and encapsulate access to a data source, such as a persistent database or an in-memory database.

The downside of this approach is that this kind of cohesion can group multiple concerns together, which introduces additional dependencies for a class that only uses and requires some of the operations.

Utility

You may be tempted to group different unrelated methods inside a class. This happens when it is not obvious where the methods belong so you end up with a utility class that is a bit like a jack of all trades.

This is generally to be avoided because you end up with low cohesion. The methods are not related, so the class as a whole is harder to reason about. In addition, utility classes exhibit a poor discoverability characteristic. You want your code to be easy to find and easy to understand how it is supposed to be used. Utility classes go against this principle because they contain different methods that are unrelated without a clear categorization.

Logical

Say you needed to provide implementations for parsing from CSV, JSON, and XML. You may be tempted to group the methods responsible for parsing the different format inside one class, as shown in Example 2-10.

Example 2-10. An example of logical cohesion

```java
public class BankTransactionParser {

    public BankTransaction parseFromCSV(final String line) {
        // ...
        throw new UnsupportedOperationException();
    }

    public BankTransaction parseFromJSON(final String line) {
        // ...
        throw new UnsupportedOperationException();
    }

    public BankTransaction parseFromXML(final String line) {
        // ...
        throw new UnsupportedOperationException();
    }
}
```

In fact, the methods are logically categorized to do "parsing." However, they are different by nature and each of the methods would be unrelated. Grouping them would also break the SRP, which you learned about earlier, because the class is responsible for multiple concerns. Consequently, this approach is not recommended.

You will learn in "Coupling" on page 21 that there exist techniques to solve the problem of providing different implementations for parsing while also keeping high cohesion.

Sequential

Say you need to read a file, parse it, process it, and save the information. You may group all of the methods in one single class. After all the output of reading the file becomes the input to the parsing, the output of parsing becomes the input to the processing step, and so on.

This is called sequential cohesion because you are grouping the methods so that they follow a sequence of input to output. It makes it easy to understand how the operations work together. Unfortunately, in practice this means that the class grouping the methods has multiple reasons to change and is therefore breaking the SRP. In addition, there may be many different ways of processing, summarizing, and saving, so this technique quickly leads to complex classes.

A better approach is to break down each responsibility inside individual, cohesive classes.

Temporal

A temporally cohesive class is one that performs several operations that are only related in time. A typical example is a class that declares some sort of initialization and clean-up operations (e.g., connecting and closing a database connection) that is called before or after other processing operations. The initialization and the other operations are unrelated, but they have to be called in a specific order in time.

Table 2-1. Summary of pros and cons for different levels of cohesion

Level of cohesion	Pro	Con
Functional (high cohesion)	Easy to understand	Can lead to overly simplistic classes
Informational (medium cohesion)	Easy to maintain	Can lead to unnecessary dependencies
Sequential (medium cohesion)	Easy to locate related operations	Encourages violation of SRP
Logical (medium cohesion)	Provides some form of high-level categorization	Encourages violation of SRP
Utility (low cohesion)	Simple to put in place	Harder to reason about the responsibility of the class
Temporal (low cohesion)	N/A	Harder to understand and use individual operations

Method-Level Cohesion

The same principle of cohesion can be applied to methods. The more different functionalities a method performs, the harder it becomes to understand what that method actually does. In other words, your method has low cohesion if it is handling multiple unrelated concerns. Methods that display low cohesion are also harder to test because they have multiple responsibilities within one method, which makes it difficult to test the responsibilities individually! Typically, if you find yourself with a method that contains a series of if/else blocks that make modifications to many different fields of a class or parameters to the method, then it is a sign you should break down the method in more cohesive parts.

Coupling

Another important characteristic about the code you write is *coupling*. Where *cohesion* is about how related things are in a class, package, or method, *coupling* is about how dependent you are on other classes. Another way to think about coupling is how much knowledge (i.e., specific implementation) you rely on about certain classes. This is important because the more classes you rely on, the less flexible you become when introducing changes. In fact, the class affected by a change may affect all the classes depending on it.

To understand what coupling is, think about a clock. There is no need to know how a clock works to read the time, so you are not dependent on the clock internals. This means you could change the clock internals without affecting how to read the time. Those two concerns (interface and implementation) are decoupled from one another.

Coupling is concerned with *how dependent* things are. For example, so far the class `BankStatementAnalyzer` relies on the class `BankStatementCSVParser`. What if you need to change the parser so it supports statements encoded as JSON entries? What about XML entries? This would be an annoying refactoring! But do not worry, you can decouple different components by using an interface, which is the tool of choice for providing flexibility for changing requirements.

First, you need to introduce an interface that will tell you how you can use a parser for bank statements but without hardcoding a specific implementation, as shown in Example 2-11.

Example 2-11. Introducing an interface for parsing bank statements

```
public interface BankStatementParser {
    BankTransaction parseFrom(String line);
    List<BankTransaction> parseLinesFrom(List<String> lines);
}
```

Your `BankStatementCSVParser` will now become an implementation of that interface:

```
public class BankStatementCSVParser implements BankStatementParser {
    // ...
}
```

So far so good, but how do you decouple the `BankStatementAnalyzer` from the specific implementation of a `BankStatementCSVParser`? You need to use the interface! By introducing a new method called `analyze()`, which takes `BankTransaction Parser` as an argument, you are no longer coupled to a specific implementation (see Example 2-12).

Example 2-12. Decoupling the Bank Statements Analyzer from the parser

```
public class BankStatementAnalyzer {
    private static final String RESOURCES = "src/main/resources/";

    public void analyze(final String fileName, final BankStatementParser bankState
mentParser)
    throws IOException {

        final Path path = Paths.get(RESOURCES + fileName);
        final List<String> lines = Files.readAllLines(path);

        final List<BankTransaction> bankTransactions = bankStatementParser.parseLi
nesFrom(lines);

        final BankStatementProcessor bankStatementProcessor = new BankStatementPro
cessor(bankTransactions);

        collectSummary(bankStatementProcessor);
    }

    // ...
}
```

This is great because the `BankStatementAnalyzer` class no longer requires knowledge of different specific implementations, which helps with coping for changing requirements. Figure 2-1 illustrates the difference of dependencies when you decouple two classes.

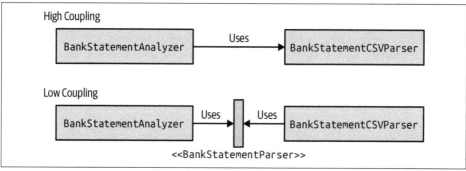

Figure 2-1. Decoupling two classes

You can now bring all the different parts together and create your main application, as shown in Example 2-13.

Example 2-13. The main application to run

```java
public class MainApplication {

    public static void main(final String... args) throws IOException {

        final BankStatementAnalyzer bankStatementAnalyzer
                = new BankStatementAnalyzer();

        final BankStatementParser bankStatementParser
                = new BankStatementCSVParser();

        bankStatementAnalyzer.analyze(args[0], bankStatementParser);

    }
}
```

Generally, when writing code you will aim for *low coupling*. This means that different components in your code are not relying on internal/implementation details. The opposite of low coupling is called *high coupling*, which is what you definitely want to avoid!

Testing

You have written some software and it looks like things are working if you execute your application a couple of times. However, how confident are you that your code will always work? What guarantee can you give your client that you have met the requirements? In this section, you will learn about testing and how to write your first automated test using the most popular and widely adopted Java testing framework: JUnit.

Automated Testing

Automated testing sounds like yet another thing that could take more time away from the fun part, which is writing code! Why should you care?

Unfortunately in software development, things never work the first time. It should be pretty obvious that testing has benefits. Can you imagine integrating a new auto-pilot software for planes without testing if the software actually works?

Testing does not have to be a manual operation, though. In automated testing you have a suite of tests that runs automatically without human intervention. This means the tests can be executed quickly when you are introducing changes in the code and you want to increase confidence that the behavior of your software is correct and has not suddenly become unexpected. On an average day, a professional developer will often run hundreds or thousands of automated tests.

In this section, we will first briefly review the benefits of automated testing so you have a clear understanding of why testing is a core part of good software development.

Confidence

First, performing tests on the software to validate whether the behavior matches the specification gives you confidence that you have met the requirements of your client. You can present the test specifications and results to your client as a guarantee. In a sense, the tests become the specification from your client.

Robustness to changes

Second, if you introduce changes to your code, how do you know that you have not accidentally broken something? If the code is small you may think problems will be obvious. However, what if you are working on a codebase with millions of lines of code? How confident would you feel about making changes to a colleague's code? Having a suite of automated tests is very useful to check that you have not introduced new bugs.

Program comprehension

Third, automated tests can be useful to help you understand how the different components inside the source code project works. In fact, tests make explicit the dependencies of different components and how they interact together. This can be extremely useful for quickly getting an overview of your software. Say you are assigned to a new project. Where would you start to get an overview of different components? The tests are a great place to start.

Using JUnit

Hopefully you are now convinced of the value of writing automated tests. In this section, you will learn how to create your first automated test using a popular Java framework called *JUnit*. Nothing comes for free. You will see that writing a test takes time. In addition, you will have to think about the longer-term maintenance of the test you write since it is regular code, after all. However, the benefits listed in the previous section far outweigh the downsides of having to write tests. Specifically, you will write *unit tests*, which verify a small isolated unit of behavior for correctness, such as a method or a small class. Throughout the book you will learn about guidelines for writing good tests. Here you will first get an initial overview for writing a simple test for the BankTransactionCSVParser.

Defining a test method

The first question is where do you write your test? The standard convention from the Maven and Gradle build tools is to include your code in *src/main/java* and the test classes inside *src/test/java*. You will also need to add a dependency to the JUnit library to your project. You will learn more about how to structure a project using Maven and Gradle in Chapter 3.

Example 2-14 shows a simple test for BankTransactionCSVParser.

> Our BankStatementCSVParserTest test class has the Test suffix. It is not strictly necessary, but often used as a useful aide memoire.

Example 2-14. A failing unit test for the CSV parser

```
import org.junit.Assert;
import org.junit.Test;
public class BankStatementCSVParserTest {

    private final BankStatementParser statementParser = new BankStatementCSV
Parser();

    @Test
    public void shouldParseOneCorrectLine() throws Exception {
        Assert.fail("Not yet implemented");
    }

}
```

There are a lot of new parts here. Let's break it down:

- The unit test class is an ordinary class called BankStatementCSVParserTest. It is a common convention to use the Test suffix at the end of test class names.
- The class declares one method: shouldParseOneCorrectLine(). It is recommended to always come up with a descriptive name so it is immediately obvious what the unit test does without looking at the implementation of the test method.
- This method is annotated with the JUnit annotation @Test. This means that the method represents a unit test that should be executed. You can declare private helper methods with a test class, but they won't be executed by the test runner.
- The implementation of this method calls Assert.fail("Not yet imple mented"), which will cause the unit test to fail with the diagnostic message "Not

yet implemented". You will learn shortly how to actually implement a unit test using a set of assertion operations available in JUnit.

You can execute your test directly from your favorite build tool (e.g., Maven or Gradle) or by using your IDE. For example, after running the test in the IntelliJ IDE, you get the output in Figure 2-2. You can see the test is failing with the diagnostic "Not yet implemented". Let's now see how to actually implement a useful test to increase the confidence that the `BankStatementCSVParser` works correctly.

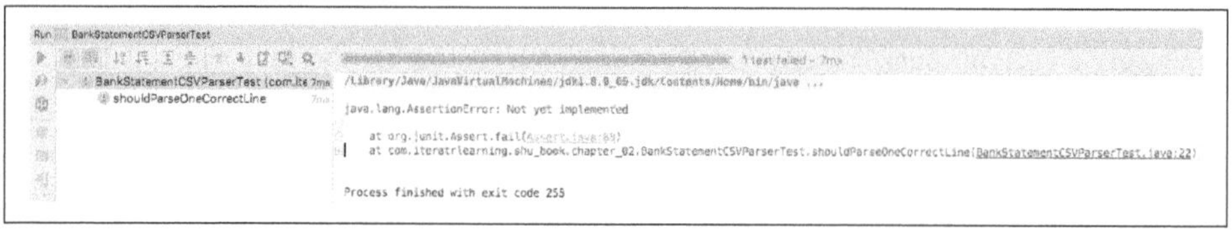

Figure 2-2. Screenshot from the IntelliJ IDE of running a failing unit test

Assert statements

You have just learned about `Assert.fail()`. This is a static method provided by JUnit called an *assert statement*. JUnit provides many assert statements to test for certain conditions. They let you provide an expected result and compare it with the result of some operation.

One of these static method is called `Assert.assertEquals()`. You can use it as shown in Example 2-15 to test that the implementation of `parseFrom()` works correctly for a particular input.

Example 2-15. Using assertion statements

```
@Test
public void shouldParseOneCorrectLine() throws Exception {
    final String line = "30-01-2017,-50,Tesco";

    final BankTransaction result = statementParser.parseFrom(line);

    final BankTransaction expected
        = new BankTransaction(LocalDate.of(2017, Month.JANUARY, 30), -50, "Tesco");
    final double tolerance = 0.0d;

    Assert.assertEquals(expected.getDate(), result.getDate());
    Assert.assertEquals(expected.getAmount(), result.getAmount(), tolerance);
    Assert.assertEquals(expected.getDescription(), result.getDescription());
}
```

So what is going on here? There are three parts:

1. You set up the context for your test. In this case a line to parse.

2. You carry out an action. In this case, you parse the input line.

3. You specify assertions of the expected output. Here, you check that the date, amount, and description were parsed correctly.

This three-stage pattern for setting up a unit test is often referred to as the *Given-When-Then* formula. It is a good idea to follow the pattern and split up the different parts because it helps to clearly understand what the test is actually doing.

When you run the test again, with a bit luck you will see a nice green bar indicating that the test succeeded, as shown in Figure 2-3.

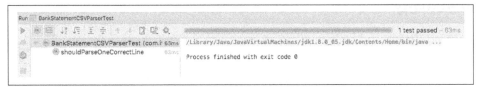

Figure 2-3. Running a passing unit test

There are other assertion statements available, which are summarized in Table 2-2.

Table 2-2. Assertion statements

Assertion statement	Purpose
`Assert.fail(message)`	Let the method fail. This is useful as a placeholder before you implement the test code.
`Assert.assertEquals (expected, actual)`	Test that two values are the same.
`Assert.assertEquals (expected, actual, delta)`	Assert that two floats or doubles are equal to within a delta.
`Assert.assertNotNull(object)`	Assert that an object is not null.

Code Coverage

You've written your first test and it's great! But how can you tell if that is sufficient? *Code coverage* refers to how much of the source code of your software (i.e., how many lines or blocks) is tested by a set of tests. It is generally a good idea to aim for high coverage because it reduces the chance of unexpected bugs. There isn't a specific percentage that is considered sufficient, but we recommend aiming for 70%–90%. In practice, it is hard and less practical to actually reach 100% of code coverage because you may, for example, start testing getter and setter methods, which provides less value.

However, code coverage is not necessarily a good metric of how well you are testing your software. In fact, code coverage only tells you what you definitely have not tested. Code coverage does not say anything about the quality of your tests. You may cover parts of your code with a simplistic test case, but not necessarily for edge cases, which usually lead to problematic issues.

Popular code coverage tools in Java include *JaCoCo*, *Emma*, and *Cobertura*. In practice, you will see people talking about line coverage, which tells you how many statements the code covered. This technique gives a false sense of having good coverage because conditionals (if, while, for) will count as one statement. However, conditionals have multiple possible paths. You should therefore favor *branch coverage*, which checks the true and false branch for each conditional.

Takeaways

- God Classes and code duplication lead to code that is hard to reason about and maintain.
- The Single Responsibility Principle helps you write code that is easier to manage and maintain.
- Cohesion is concerned with how how strongly related the responsibilities of a class or method are.
- Coupling is concerned with how dependent a class is on other parts of your code.
- High cohesion and low coupling are characteristics of maintainable code.
- A suite of automated tests increases confidence that your software is correct, makes it more robust for changes, and helps program comprehension.
- JUnit is a Java testing framework that lets you specify unit tests that verify the behavior of your methods and classes.
- Given-When-Then is a pattern for setting up a test into three parts to help understand the tests you implement.

Iterating on You

If you want to extend and solidify the knowledge from this section, you could try one of these activities:

- Write a couple more unit test cases to test the implementation of the CSV parser.
- Support different aggregate operations, such as finding the maximum or minimum transactions in specific date ranges.

- Return a histogram of the expenses by grouping them based on months and descriptions.

Completing the Challenge

Mark Erbergzuck is very happy with your first iteration of your Bank Statements Analyzer. He takes your idea and renames it **THE Bank Statements Analyzer**. He is so happy with your application that he is asking you for a few enhancements. It turns out he would like to extend the reading, parsing, processing, and summarizing functionalities. For example, he is a fan of JSON. In addition, he found your tests a bit limited and found a couple of bugs.

This is something that you will address in the next chapter, where you will learn about exception handling, the Open/Closed Principle, and how to build your Java project using a build tool.

CHAPTER 3

Extending the Bank Statements Analyzer

The Challenge

Mark Erbergzuck was very happy with the work you did in the previous chapter. You built a basic Bank Statements Analyzer as a minimum viable product. Because of this success Mark Erbergzuck thinks that your product can be taken further and asks you to build a new version that support multiple features.

The Goal

In the previous chapter, you learned how to create an application to analyze bank statements in a CSV format. Along this journey you learned about core design principles that help you write maintainable code, the Single Responsibility Principle, and anti-patterns you should avoid, such as God Class and code duplication. While you were incrementally refactoring your code you also learned about coupling (how dependent you are on other classes) and cohesion (how related things are in a class).

Nonetheless, the application is currently pretty limited. How about providing functionality for searching for different kinds of transactions, supporting multiple formats, processors, and exporting the results into a nice report with different formats such as text and HTML?

In this chapter, you will go deeper in your software development quest. First, you will learn about the Open/Closed principle, which is essential for adding flexibility to your codebase and improving code maintenance. You will also learn general guidelines for when it makes sense to introduce interfaces, as well as other gotchas to avoid high coupling. You will also learn about the use of exceptions in Java—when it makes sense to include them as part of the APIs you define and when it doesn't. Finally, you will learn how to systematically build a Java project using an established build tool like Maven and Gradle.

 If at any point you want to look at the source code for this chapter, you can look at the package com.iteratrlearning.shu_book.chap ter_03 in the book's code repository.

Extended Bank Statements Analyzer Requirements

You had a friendly chat with Mark Erbergzuck to collect new requirements for the second iteration of the Bank Statements Analyzer. He would like to extend the functionality of the kind of operations you can perform. At the moment the application is limited, as it can only query for the revenue in a particular month or category. Mark has requested two new functionalities:

1. He'd like to also be able to search for specific transactions. For example, you should be able to return all the bank transactions in a given date range or for a specific category.

2. Mark would like to be able to generate a report of summary statistics for his search into different formats such as text and HTML.

You will work through these requirements in order.

Open/Closed Principle

Let's start simple. You will implement a method that can find all the transactions over a certain amount. The first question is where should you declare this method? You could create a separate BankTransactionFinder class that will contain a simple find Transactions() method. However, you also declared a class BankTransactionPro cessor in the previous chapter. So what should you do? In this case, there aren't a lot of benefits in declaring a new class every time you need to add one single method. This actually adds complexity to your whole project, as it introduces a pollution of names that makes it harder to understand the relationships between these different behaviors. Declaring the method inside BankTransactionProcessor helps with discoverability as you immediately know that this is the class that groups all methods that do some form of processing. Now that you've decided where to declare it, you can implement it as shown in Example 3-1.

Example 3-1. Find bank transactions over a certain amount

```java
public List<BankTransaction> findTransactionsGreaterThanEqual(final int amount) {
    final List<BankTransaction> result = new ArrayList<>();
    for(final BankTransaction bankTransaction: bankTransactions) {
        if(bankTransaction.getAmount() >= amount) {
            result.add(bankTransaction);
        }
    }
    return result;
}
```

This code is reasonable. However, what if you want to also search in a certain month? You need to duplicate this method as shown in Example 3-2.

Example 3-2. Find bank transactions in a certain month

```java
public List<BankTransaction> findTransactionsInMonth(final Month month) {
    final List<BankTransaction> result = new ArrayList<>();
    for(final BankTransaction bankTransaction: bankTransactions) {
        if(bankTransaction.getDate().getMonth() == month) {
            result.add(bankTransaction);
        }
    }
    return result;
}
```

In the previous chapter, you already came across code duplication. It is a code smell which leads to code that is brittle, especially if requirements change frequently. For example, if the iteration logic needs to change, you will need to repeat the modifications in several places.

This approach also doesn't work well for more complicated requirements. What if we wish to search transactions in a specific month and also over a certain amount? You could implement this new requirement as shown in Example 3-3.

Example 3-3. Find bank transactions in a certain month and over a certain amount

```java
public List<BankTransaction> findTransactionsInMonthAndGreater(final Month month,
final int amount) {
    final List<BankTransaction> result = new ArrayList<>();
    for(final BankTransaction bankTransaction: bankTransactions) {
        if(bankTransaction.getDate().getMonth() == month && bankTransaction.getA
mount() >= amount) {
            result.add(bankTransaction);
        }
    }
    return result;
}
```

Clearly this approach exhibits several downsides:

- Your code will become increasingly complicated as you have to combine multiple properties of a bank transaction.
- The selection logic is coupled to the iteration logic, making it harder to separate them out.
- You keep on duplicating code.

This is where the Open/Closed principle comes in. It promotes the idea of being able to change the behavior of a method or class without having to modify the code. In our example, it would mean the ability to extend the behavior of a findTransac tions() method without having to duplicate the code or change it to introduce a new parameter. How is this possible? As discussed earlier, the concepts of iterating and the business logic are coupled together. In the previous chapter, you learned about interfaces as a useful tool to decouple concepts from one another. In this case, you will introduce a BankTransactionFilter interface that will be responsible for the selection logic, as shown in Example 3-4. It contains a single method test() that returns a boolean and takes the complete BankTransaction object as an argument. This way the method test() has access to all the properties of a BankTransaction to specify any appropriate selection criteria.

 An interface that only contains a single abstract method is called a *functional interface* since Java 8. You can annotate it using the @FunctionalInterface annotation to make the intent of the interface clearer.

Example 3-4. The BankTransactionFilter interface

```
@FunctionalInterface
public interface BankTransactionFilter {
    boolean test(BankTransaction bankTransaction);
}
```

 Java 8 introduced a generic java.util.function.Predicate<T> inferface, which would be a great fit for the problem at hand. However, this chapter introduces a new named interface to avoid introducing too much complexity early on in the book.

The interface BankTransactionFilter models the concept of a selection criteria for a BankTransaction. You can now refactor the method findTransactions() to make use of it as shown in Example 3-5. This refactoring is very important because you now have introduced a way to decouple the iteration logic from the business logic through this interface. Your method no longer depends on one specific implementation of a filter. You can introduce new implementations by passing them as an argument without modifying the body of this method. Hence, it is now open for extension and closed for modification. This reduces the scope for introducing new bugs because it minimizes cascading changes required to parts of code that have already been implemented and tested. In other words, old code still works and is untouched.

Example 3-5. Flexible findTransactions() method using Open/Closed Principle

```java
public List<BankTransaction> findTransactions(final BankTransactionFilter bankTran
sactionFilter) {
    final List<BankTransaction> result = new ArrayList<>();
    for(final BankTransaction bankTransaction: bankTransactions) {
        if(bankTransactionFilter.test(bankTransaction)) {
            result.add(bankTransaction);
        }
    }
    return result;
}
```

Creating an Instance of a Functional Interface

Mark Erbergzuck is now happy as you can implement any new requirements by calling the method findTransactions() declared in the BankTransactionProcessor with appropriate implementations of a BankTransactionFilter. You can achieve this by implementing a class as shown in Example 3-6 and then passing an instance as argument to the findTransactions() method as shown in Example 3-7.

Example 3-6. Declaring a class that implements the BankTransactionFilter

```java
class BankTransactionIsInFebruaryAndExpensive implements BankTransactionFilter {

    @Override
    public boolean test(final BankTransaction bankTransaction) {
        return bankTransaction.getDate().getMonth() == Month.FEBRUARY
                && bankTransaction.getAmount() >= 1_000);
    }
}
```

Example 3-7. Calling findTransactions() with a specific implementation of BankTransactionFilter

```java
final List<BankTransaction> transactions
    = bankStatementProcessor.findTransactions(new BankTransactionIsInFebruaryAndEx
pensive());
```

Lambda Expressions

However, you'd need to create special classes every time you have a new requirement. This process can add unnecessary boilerplate and can rapidly become cumbersome. Since Java 8, you can use a feature called *lambda expressions* as shown in Example 3-8. Don't worry about this syntax and language feature for the time being. We will learn about lambda expressions and a companion language feature called *method references* in more detail in Chapter 7. For now, you can think of it as instead of passing in an object that implements an interface, we're passing in a block of code—a function without a name. bankTransaction is the name of a parameter and the arrow -> separates the parameter from the body of the lambda expression, which is just some code that is run to test whether or not the bank transaction should be selected.

Example 3-8. Implementing BankTransactionFilter using a lambda expression

```
final List<BankTransaction> transactions
    = bankStatementProcessor.findTransactions(bankTransaction ->
            bankTransaction.getDate().getMonth() == Month.FEBRUARY
            && bankTransaction.getAmount() >= 1_000);
```

To summarize, the Open/Closed Principle is a useful principle to follow because it:

- Reduces fragility of code by not changing existing code
- Promotes reusability of existing code and as a result avoids code duplication
- Promotes decoupling, which leads to better code maintenance

Interfaces Gotchas

So far you introduced a flexible method to search for transactions given a selection criterion. The refactoring you went through raises questions about what should happen to the other methods declared inside the BankTransactionProcessor class. Should they be part of an interface? Should they be included in a separate class? After all, there are three other related methods you implemented in the previous chapter:

- calculateTotalAmount()
- calculateTotalInMonth()
- calculateTotalForCategory()

One approach that we discourage you to put in practice is to put everything into one single interface: the God Interface.

God Interface

One extreme view you could take is that the class `BankTransactionProcessor` acts as an API. As a result, you may wish to define an interface that lets you decouple from multiple implementations of a bank transaction processor as shown in Example 3-9. This interface contains all the operations that the bank transaction processor needs to implement.

Example 3-9. God Interface

```
interface BankTransactionProcessor {
    double calculateTotalAmount();
    double calculateTotalInMonth(Month month);
    double calculateTotalInJanuary();
    double calculateAverageAmount();
    double calculateAverageAmountForCategory(Category category);
    List<BankTransaction> findTransactions(BankTransactionFilter bankTransactionFil
ter);
}
```

However, this approach displays several downsides. First, this interface becomes increasingly complex as every single helper operation is an integral part of the explicit API definition. Second, this interface acts more like a "God Class" as you saw in the previous chapter. In fact, the interface has now become a bag for all possible operations. Worse, you are actually introducing two forms of additional coupling:

- An interface in Java defines a contract that every single implementation has to adhere by. In other words, concrete implementations of this interface have to provide an implementation for each operation. This means that changing the interface means all concrete implementations have to be updated as well to support the change. The more operations you add, the more likely changes will happen, increasing the scope for potential problems down the line.

- Concrete properties of a `BankTransaction` such as the month and the category have cropped up as part of method names; e.g., `calculateAverageForCate gory()` and `calculateTotalInJanuary()`. This is more problematic with interfaces as they now depend on specific accessors of a domain object. If the internals of that domain object change, then this may cause changes to the interface as well and, as a consequence, to all its concrete implementations, too.

All these reasons are why it is generally recommended to define smaller interfaces. The idea is to minimize dependency to multiple operations or internals of a domain object.

Too Granular

Since we've just argued that smaller is better, the other extreme view you could take is to define one interface for each operation, as shown in Example 3-10. Your `BankTran sactionProcessor` class would implement all these interfaces.

Example 3-10. Interfaces that are too granular

```
interface CalculateTotalAmount {
    double calculateTotalAmount();
}

interface CalculateAverage {
    double calculateAverage();
}

interface CalculateTotalInMonth {
    double calculateTotalInMonth(Month month);
}
```

This approach is also not useful for improving code maintenance. In fact, it introduces "anti-cohesion." In other words, it becomes harder to discover the operations of interest as they are hiding in multiple separate interfaces. Part of promoting good maintenance is to help discoverability of common operations. In addition, because the interfaces are too granular it adds overall complexity, as well as a lot of different new types introduced by the new interfaces to keep track of in your project.

Explicit Versus Implicit API

So what is the pragmatic approach to take? We recommend following the Open/Closed Principle to add flexibility to your operations and define the most common cases as part of the class. They can be implemented with the more general methods. In this scenario, an interface is not particularly warranted as we don't expect different implementations of a `BankTransactionProcessor`. There aren't specializations of each of these methods that will benefit your overall application. As a result, there's no need to over-engineer and add unnecessary abstractions in your codebase. The `Bank TransactionProcessor` is simply a class that lets you perform statistical operations on bank transactions.

This also raises the question of whether methods such as `findTransactionsGreater ThanEqual()` should be declared given that they can easily be implemented by the more general `findTransactions()` method. This dilemma is often referred to as the problem of providing an explicit versus implicit API.

In fact, there are two sides of the coin to consider. On one side a method like `find TransactionsGreaterThanEqual()` is self-explanatory and easy to use. You should not be worried about adding descriptive method names to help readability and comprehension of your API. However, this method is restricted to a particular case and you can easily have an explosion of new methods to cater for various multiple requirements. On the other side, a method like findTransactions() is initially more difficult to use and it needs to be well-documented. However, it provides a unified API for all cases where you need to look up transactions. There isn't a rule of what is best; it depends on what kind of queries you expect. If findTransactionsGreaterTha nEqual() is a very common operation, it makes sense to extract it into an explicit API to make it easier for users to understand and use.

The final implementation of the BankTransactionProcessor is shown in Example 3-11.

Example 3-11. Key operations for the BankTransactionProcessor class

```java
@FunctionalInterface
public interface BankTransactionSummarizer {
    double summarize(double accumulator, BankTransaction bankTransaction);
}



@FunctionalInterface
public interface BankTransactionFilter {
    boolean test(BankTransaction bankTransaction);
}

public class BankTransactionProcessor {

    private final List<BankTransaction> bankTransactions;

    public BankStatementProcessor(final List<BankTransaction> bankTransactions) {
        this.bankTransactions = bankTransactions;
    }

    public double summarizeTransactions(final BankTransactionSummarizer bankTransac
tionSummarizer) {
        double result = 0;
        for(final BankTransaction bankTransaction: bankTransactions) {
            result = bankTransactionSummarizer.summarize(result, bankTransaction);
        }
        return result;
    }

    public double calculateTotalInMonth(final Month month) {
        return summarizeTransactions((acc, bankTransaction) ->
                bankTransaction.getDate().getMonth() == month ? acc  + bankTransac
tion.getAmount() : acc
        );
    }
```

```
    // ...

    public List<BankTransaction> findTransactions(final BankTransactionFilter bank
TransactionFilter) {
        final List<BankTransaction> result = new ArrayList<>();
        for(final BankTransaction bankTransaction: bankTransactions) {
            if(bankTransactionFilter.test(bankTransaction)) {
                result.add(bankTransaction);
            }
        }
        return bankTransactions;
    }

    public List<BankTransaction> findTransactionsGreaterThanEqual(final int amount)
{
        return findTransactions(bankTransaction -> bankTransaction.getAmount() >=
amount);
    }

    // ...
}
```

A lot of the aggregation patterns that you have seen so far could be implemented using the Streams API introduced in Java 8 if you are familiar with it. For example, searching for transactions can be easily specified as shown here:

```
bankTransactions
    .stream()
    .filter(bankTransaction -> bankTransaction.getA
mount() >= 1_000)
    .collect(toList());
```

Nonetheless, the Streams API is implemented using the same foundation and principles that you've learned in this section.

Domain Class or Primitive Value?

While we kept the interface definition of BankTransactionSummarizer simple, it is often preferable to not return a primitive value like a double if you are looking at returning a result from an aggregation. This is because it doesn't give you the flexibility to later return multiple results. For example, the method summarizeTransac tion() returns a double. If you were to change the signature of the result to include more results, you would need to change every single implementation of the BankTran sactionProcessor.

A solution to this problem is to introduce a new domain class such as Summary that wraps the double value. This means that in the future you can add other fields and results to this class. This technique helps further decouple the various concepts in your domain and also helps minimize cascading changes when requirements change.

 A primitive `double` value has a limited number of bits, and as a result it has limited precision when storing decimal numbers. An alternative to consider is `java.math.BigDecimal`, which has arbitrary precision. However, this precision comes at the cost of increased CPU and memory overhead.

Multiple Exporters

In the previous section you learned about the Open/Closed Principle and delved further into the usage of interfaces in Java. This knowledge is going to come handy as Mark Erbergzuck has a new requirement! You need to export summary statistics about a selected list of transactions into different formats including text, HTML, JSON, and so on. Where to start?

Introducing a Domain Object

First, you need to define exactly what is it the user wants to export. There are various possibilities, which we explore together with their trade-offs:

A number
> Perhaps the user is just interested in returning the result of an operation like `cal culateAverageInMonth`. This means the result would be a `double`. While this is the most simple approach, as we noted earlier, this approach is somewhat inflexible as it doesn't cope well with changing requirements. Imagine you create an exporter which takes the `double` as an input, this means that every places in your code that calls this exporter will need to be updated if you need to change the result type, possibly introducing new bugs.

A collection
> Perhaps the user wishes to return a list of transactions, for example, returned by `findTransaction()`. You could even return an `Iterable` to provide further flexibility in what specific implementation is returned. While this gives you more flexibility it also ties you to only being able to return a collection. What if you need to return multiple results such as a list and other summary information?

A specialized domain object
> You could introduce a new concept such as `SummaryStatistics` which represents summary information that the user is interested in exporting. A *domain object* is simply an instance of a class that is related to your domain. By introducing a domain object, you introduce a form of decoupling. In fact, if there are new requirements where you need to export additional information, you can just

include it as part of this new class without having to introduce cascading changes.

A more complex domain object

You could introduce a concept such as Report which is more generic and could contain different kinds of fields storing various results including collection of transactions. Whether you need this or not depends on the user requirements and whether you are expecting more complex information. The benefit again is that you are able to decouple different parts of your applications that produce Report objects and other parts that consume Report objects.

For the purpose of our application, let's introduce a domain object that stores summary statistics about a list of transactions. The code in Example 3-12 shows its declaration.

Example 3-12. A domain object storing statistical information

```java
public class SummaryStatistics {

    private final double sum;
    private final double max;
    private final double min;
    private final double average;

    public SummaryStatistics(final double sum, final double max, final double min,
final double average) {
        this.sum = sum;
        this.max = max;
        this.min = min;
        this.average = average;
    }

    public double getSum() {
        return sum;
    }

    public double getMax() {
        return max;
    }

    public double getMin() {
        return min;
    }

    public double getAverage() {
        return average;
    }
}
```

Defining and Implementing the Appropriate Interface

Now that you know what you need to export, you will come up with an API to do it. You will need to define an interface called `Exporter`. The reason you introduce an interface is to let you decouple from multiple implementations of exporters. This goes in line with the Open/Closed Principle you learned in the previous section. In fact, if you need to substitute the implementation of an exporter to JSON with an exporter to XML this will be straightforward given they will both implement the same interface. Your first attempt at defining the interface may be as shown in Example 3-13. The method `export()` takes a `SummaryStatistics` object and returns void.

Example 3-13. Bad Exporter interface

```
public interface Exporter {
    void export(SummaryStatistics summaryStatistics);
}
```

This approach is to be avoided for several reasons:

- The return type `void` is not useful and is difficult to reason about. You don't know what is returned. The signature of the `export()` method implies that some state change is happening somewhere or that this method will log or print information back to the screen. We don't know!

- Returning `void` makes it very hard to test the result with assertions. What is the actual result to compare with the expected result? Unfortunately, you can't get a result with `void`.

With this in mind, you come up with an alternative API that returns a `String`, as shown in Example 3-14. It is now clear that the `Exporter` will return text and it's then up to a separate part of the program to decide whether to print it, save it to a file, or even send it electronically. Text strings are also very useful for testing as you can directly compare them with assertions.

Example 3-14. Good Exporter interface

```
public interface Exporter {
    String export(SummaryStatistics summaryStatistics);
}
```

Now that you have defined an API to export information, you can implement various kinds of exporters that respect the contract of the `Exporter` interface. You can see an example of implementing a basic HTML exporter in Example 3-15.

Example 3-15. Implementing the Exporter interface

```
public class HtmlExporter implements Exporter {
    @Override
    public String export(final SummaryStatistics summaryStatistics) {

        String result = "<!doctype html>";
        result += "<html lang='en'>";
        result += "<head><title>Bank Transaction Report</title></head>";
        result += "<body>";
        result += "<ul>";
        result += "<li><strong>The sum is</strong>: " + summaryStatistics.getSum()
+ "</li>";
        result += "<li><strong>The average is</strong>: " + summaryStatistics.getA
verage() + "</li>";
        result += "<li><strong>The max is</strong>: " + summaryStatistics.getMax()
+ "</li>";
        result += "<li><strong>The min is</strong>: " + summaryStatistics.getMin()
+ "</li>";
        result += "</ul>";
        result += "</body>";
        result += "</html>";
        return result;
    }
}
```

Exception Handling

So far we've not talked about what happens when things go wrong. Can you think of situations where the bank analyzer software might fail? For example:

- What if the data cannot be parsed properly?
- What if the CSV file containing the bank transctions to import can't be read?
- What if the hardware running your applications runs out of resources such as RAM or disk space?

In these scenarios you will be welcomed with a scary error message that includes a stack trace showing the origin of the problem. The snippets in Example 3-16 show examples of these unexpected errors.

Example 3-16. Unexpected problems

```
Exception in thread "main" java.lang.ArrayIndexOutOfBoundsException: 0

Exception in thread "main" java.nio.file.NoSuchFileException: src/main/resources/
bank-data-simple.csv

Exception in thread "main" java.lang.OutOfMemoryError: Java heap space
```

Why Use Exceptions?

Let's focus on the `BankStatementCSVParser` for the moment. How do we handle parsing problems? For example, a CSV line in the file might not be written in the expected format:

- A CSV line may have more than the expected three columns.
- A CSV line may have fewer than the expected three columns.
- The data format of some of the columns may not be correct, e.g., the date may be incorrect.

Back in the frightening days of the C programming language, you would add a lot of if-condition checks that would return a cryptic error code. This approach had several drawbacks. First, it relied on global shared mutable state to look up the most recent error. This made it harder to understand individual parts of your code in isolation. As a result, your code became harder to maintain. Second, this approach was error prone as you needed to distinguish between real values and errors encoded as values. The type system in this case was weak and could be more helpful to the programmer. Finally, the control flow was mixed with the business logic, which contributed to making the code harder to maintain and test in isolation.

To solve these issues, Java incorporated exceptions as a first-class language feature that introduced many benefits:

Documentation
The language supports exceptions as part of method signatures.

Type safety
The type system figures out whether you are handling the exceptional flow.

Separation of concern
Business logic and exception recovery are separated out with a try/catch block.

The problem is that exceptions as a language feature also add more complexity. You may be familiar with the fact that Java distinguishes between two kinds of exceptions:

Checked exceptions
These are errors that you are expected to be able to recover from. In Java, you have to declare a method with a list of checked exceptions it can throw. If not, you have to provide a suitable try/catch block for that particular exception.

Unchecked exceptions
These are errors that can be thrown at any time during the program execution. Methods don't have to explicitly declare these exceptions in their signature and the caller doesn't have to handle them explicitly, as it would with a checked exception.

Java exception classes are organized in a well-defined hierarchy. Figure 3-1 depicts that hierarchy in Java. The `Error` and `RuntimeException` classes are unchecked exceptions and are subclasses of `Throwable`. You shouldn't expect to catch and recover from them. The class `Exception` typically represents errors that a program should be able to recover from.

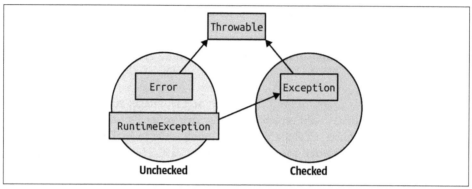

Figure 3-1. Exceptions hierarchy in Java

Patterns and Anti-Patterns with Exceptions

Which category of exceptions should you use under what scenario? You may also wonder how should you update the `BankStatementParser` API to support exceptions. Unfortunately, there isn't a simple answer. It requires a bit of pragmatism when deciding what is the right approach for you.

There are two separate concerns when thinking about parsing the CSV file:

- Parsing the right syntax (e.g., CSV, JSON)
- Validation of the data (e.g., text description should be less than 100 characters)

You will focus on the syntax error first and then the validation of the data.

Deciding between unchecked and checked

There are situations when the CSV file may not follow the correct syntax (for example, if separating commas are missing). Ignoring this problem will lead to confusing errors when the application runs. Part of the benefit of supporting exceptions in your code is to provide a clearer diagnosis to the user of your API in the event that a problem arises. Accordingly, you decide to add a simple check as shown in the code in Example 3-17, which throws a `CSVSyntaxException`.

Example 3-17. Throwing a syntax exception

```
final String[] columns = line.split(",");

if(columns.length < EXPECTED_ATTRIBUTES_LENGTH) {
    throw new CSVSyntaxException();
}
```

Should `CSVSyntaxException` be a checked or an unchecked exception? To answer this question you need to ask yourself whether you require the user of your API to take a compulsory recovery action. For example, the user may implement a retry mechanism if it is a transient error or she may display a message back on the screen to add graceful responsiveness to the application. Typically, errors due to business logic validation (e.g., wrong format or arithmetic) should be unchecked exceptions, as they would add a lot of try/catch clutter in your code. It may also not be obvious what the right recovery mechanism is. Consequently, there's no point enforcing it on the user of your API. In addition, system errors (e.g., disk ran out of space) should also be unchecked exceptions as there's nothing the client can do. In a nutshell, the recommendation is to use unchecked exceptions and only use checked exceptions sparingly to avoid significant clutter in the code.

Let's now tackle the problem of validating the data once you know it follows the correct CSV format. You will learn about two common anti-patterns with using exceptions for validation. Then, you will learn about the Notification pattern, which provides a maintainable solution to the problem.

Overly specific

The first question going through your mind is where should you add validation logic? You could have it right at the construction time of the `BankStatement` object. However, we recommend creating a dedicated `Validator` class for several reasons:

- You don't have to duplicate the validation logic when you need to reuse it.
- You get confidence that different parts of your system validate the same way.
- You can easily unit test this logic separately.
- It follows the SRP, which leads to simpler maintenance and program comprehension.

The are various approaches to implementing your validator using exceptions. One overly specific approach is shown in Example 3-18. You have thought of every single edge case to validate the input and converted each edge case into a checked exception. The exceptions `DescriptionTooLongException`, `InvalidDateFormat`, `DateInTheFu tureException`, and `InvalidAmountException` are all user-defined checked exceptions (i.e., they extend the class `Exception`). While this approach lets you specify precise recovery mechanisms for each exception, it is clearly unproductive as it requires a lot of setup, declares multiple exceptions, and forces the user to explicitly deal with each of these exceptions. This is doing the opposite of helping the user understand and simply use your API. In addition, you can't collect all the errors as a whole in case you want to provide a list to the user.

Example 3-18. Overly specific exceptions

```java
public class OverlySpecificBankStatementValidator {

    private String description;
    private String date;
    private String amount;

    public OverlySpecificBankStatementValidator(final String description, final
String date, final String amount) {
        this.description = Objects.requireNonNull(description);
        this.date = Objects.requireNonNull(description);
        this.amount = Objects.requireNonNull(description);
    }

    public boolean validate() throws DescriptionTooLongException,
                                     InvalidDateFormat,
                                     DateInTheFutureException,
                                     InvalidAmountException {

        if(this.description.length() > 100) {
            throw new DescriptionTooLongException();
        }

        final LocalDate parsedDate;
        try {
            parsedDate = LocalDate.parse(this.date);
        }
        catch (DateTimeParseException e) {
            throw new InvalidDateFormat();
        }
        if (parsedDate.isAfter(LocalDate.now())) throw new DateInTheFutureExcep
tion();

        try {
            Double.parseDouble(this.amount);
        }
        catch (NumberFormatException e) {
            throw new InvalidAmountException();
        }
        return true;
    }
}
```

Overly apathetic

The other end of the spectrum is making everything an unchecked exception; for example, by using `IllegalArgumentException`. The code in Example 3-19 shows the implementation of the `validate()` method following this approach. The problem with this approach is that you can't have specific recovery logic because all the exceptions are the same! In addition, you still can't collect all the errors as a whole.

Example 3-19. IllegalArgument exceptions everywhere

```java
public boolean validate() {

    if(this.description.length() > 100) {
        throw new IllegalArgumentException("The description is too long");
    }

    final LocalDate parsedDate;
    try {
        parsedDate = LocalDate.parse(this.date);
    }
    catch (DateTimeParseException e) {
        throw new IllegalArgumentException("Invalid format for date", e);
    }
    if (parsedDate.isAfter(LocalDate.now())) throw new IllegalArgumentException("date cannot be in the future");

    try {
        Double.parseDouble(this.amount);
    }
    catch (NumberFormatException e) {
        throw new IllegalArgumentException("Invalid format for amount", e);
    }
    return true;
}
```

Next, you will learn about the Notification pattern, which provides a solution to the downsides highlighted with the overly specific and overly apathetic anti-patterns.

Notification Pattern

The Notification pattern aims to provide a solution for the situation in which you are using too many unchecked exceptions. The solution is to introduce a domain class to collect errors.[1]

The first thing you need is a `Notification` class whose responsibility is to collect errors. The code in Example 3-20 shows its declaration.

---

1 This pattern was first put forward by Martin Fowler.

Example 3-20. Introducing the domain class Notification to collect errors

```java
public class Notification {
    private final List<String> errors = new ArrayList<>();

    public void addError(final String message) {
        errors.add(message);
    }

    public boolean hasErrors() {
        return !errors.isEmpty();
    }

    public String errorMessage() {
        return errors.toString();
    }

    public List<String> getErrors() {
        return this.errors;
    }

}
```

The benefit of introducing such a class is that you can now declare a validator that is able to collect multiple errors in one pass. This wasn't possible in the two previous approaches you explored. Instead of throwing exceptions, you can now simply add messages into the Notification object as shown in Example 3-21.

Example 3-21. Notification pattern

```java
public Notification validate() {

    final Notification notification = new Notification();
    if(this.description.length() > 100) {
        notification.addError("The description is too long");
    }

    final LocalDate parsedDate;
    try {
        parsedDate = LocalDate.parse(this.date);
        if (parsedDate.isAfter(LocalDate.now())) {
            notification.addError("date cannot be in the future");
        }
    }
    catch (DateTimeParseException e) {
        notification.addError("Invalid format for date");
    }

    final double amount;
    try {
        amount = Double.parseDouble(this.amount);
```

```
    }
    catch (NumberFormatException e) {
        notification.addError("Invalid format for amount");
    }
    return notification;
}
```

Guidelines for Using Exceptions

Now that you've learned the situations for which you may use exceptions, let's discuss some general guidelines to use them effectively in your application.

Do not ignore an exception

It's never a good idea to ignore an exception as you won't be able to diagnose the root of the problem. If there isn't an obvious handling mechanism, then throw an unchecked exception instead. This way if you really need to handle the checked exception, you'll be forced to come back and deal with it after seeing the problem at runtime.

Do not catch the generic Exception

Catch a specific exception as much as you can to improve readability and support more specific exception handling. If you catch the generic Exception, it also includes a RuntimeException. Some IDEs can generate a catch clause that is too general, so you may need to think about making the catch clause more specific.

Document exceptions

Document exceptions at your API-level including unchecked exceptions to facilitate troubleshooting. In fact, unchecked exceptions report the root of an issue that should be addressed. The code in Example 3-22 shows an example of documenting exceptions using the @throws Javadoc syntax.

Example 3-22. Documenting exceptions

```
@throws  NoSuchFileException if the file does not exist
@throws  DirectoryNotEmptyException if the file is a directory and
could not otherwise be deleted because the directory is not empty
@throws  IOException if an I/O error occurs
@throws  SecurityException In the case of the default provider,
and a security manager is installed, the {@link SecurityManager#checkDelete(String)}
method is invoked to check delete access to the file
```

Watch out for implementation-specific exceptions

Do not throw implementation-specific exceptions as it breaks encapsulation of your API. For example, the definition of read() in Example 3-23 forces any future implementations to throw an OracleException, when clearly read() could support sources that are completely unrelated to Oracle!

Example 3-23. Avoid implementation-specific exceptions

```
public String read(final Source source) throws OracleException { ... }
```

Exceptions versus Control flow

Do not use exceptions for control flow. The code in Example 3-24 exemplifies a bad use of exceptions in Java. The code relies on an exception to exit the reading loop.

Example 3-24. Using exceptions for control flow

```
try {
    while (true) {
        System.out.println(source.read());
    }
}
catch(NoDataException e) {
}
```

You should avoid this type of code for several reasons. First, it leads to poor code readability because the exception try/catch syntax adds unnecessary clutter. Second, it makes the intent of your code less comprehensible. Exceptions are meant as a feature to deal with errors and exceptional scenarios. Consequently, it's good not to create an exception until you are sure that you need to throw it. Finally, there's overhead associated with holding a stack trace in the event that an exception is thrown.

Alternatives to Exceptions

You've learned about using exceptions in Java for the purpose of making your Bank Statements Analyzer more robust and comprehensible for your users. What are alternatives to exceptions, though? We briefly describe four alternative approaches together with their pros and cons.

Using null

Instead of throwing a specific exception, you may ask why you can't just return null as shown in Example 3-25.

Example 3-25. Returning null instead of an exception

```
final String[] columns = line.split(",");

if(columns.length < EXPECTED_ATTRIBUTES_LENGTH) {
    return null;
}
```

This approach is to be absolutely avoided. In fact, null provides no useful information to the caller. It is also error prone as you have to explicitly remember to check for null as a result of your API. In practice, this leads to many NullPointerExceptions and a lot of unnecessary debugging!

The Null Object pattern

An approach you sometimes see adopted in Java is the *Null Object pattern.* In a nutshell, instead of returning a null reference to convey the absence of an object, you return an object that implements the expected interface but whose method bodies are empty. The advantage of this tactic is that you won't deal with unexpected Null Pointer exceptions and a long list of null checks. In fact, this empty object is very predictable because it does nothing functionally! Nonetheless, this pattern can also be problematic because you may hide potential issues in the data with an object that simply ignores the real problem, and as a result make troubleshooting more difficult.

Optional<T>

Java 8 introduced a built-in data type java.util.Optional<T>, which is dedicated to representing the presence or absence of a value. The Optional<T> comes with a set of methods to explicitly deal with the absence of a value, which is useful to reduce the scope for bugs. It also allows you to compose various Optional objects together, which may be returned as a return type from different APIs you use. An example of that is the method findAny() in the Streams API. You will learn more about how you can use Optional<T> in Chapter 7.

Try<T>

There's another data type called Try<T>, which represents an operation that may succeed or fail. In a way it is analogous to Optional<T>, but instead of values you work with operations. In other words, the Try<T> data type brings similar code composability benefits and also helps reduce the scope for errors in your code. Unfortunately, the Try<T> data type is not built in to the JDK but is supported by external libraries that you can look at.

Using a Build Tool

So far you've learned good programming practices and principles. But what about structuring, building, and running your application? This section focuses on why using a build tool for your project is a necessity and how you can use a build tool such as Maven and Gradle to build and run your application in a predictable manner. In Chapter 5, you will learn more about a related topic of how to structure the application effectively using Java packages.

Why Use a Build Tool?

Let's consider the problem of executing your application. There are several elements you need to take care of. First, once you have written the code for your project, you will need to compile it. To do this, you will have to use the Java compiler (javac). Do you remember all the commands required to compile multiple files? What about with multiple packages? What about managing dependencies if you were to import other Java libraries? What about if the project needs to be packaged in a specific format such as WAR or JAR? Suddenly things get messy, and more and more pressure is put on the developer.

To automate all the commands required, you will need to create a script so you don't have to repeat the commands every time. Introducing a new script means that all your current and future teammates will need to be familiar with your way of thinking to be able to maintain and change the script as requirements evolve. Second, the software development life cycle needs to be taken into consideration. It's not just about developing and compiling the code. What about testing and deploying it?

The solution to these problems is using a build tool. You can think of a build tool as an assistant that can automate the repetitive tasks in the software development life cycle, including building, testing, and deploying your application. A build tool has many benefits:

- It provides you with a common structure to think about a project so your colleagues feel immediately at home with the project.

- It sets you up with a repeatable and standardized process to build and run an application.

- You spend more time on development, and less time on low-level configurations and setup.

- You are reducing the scope for introducing errors due to bad configurations or missing steps in the build.

- You save time by reusing common build tasks instead of reimplementing them.

You will now explore two popular build tools used in the Java community: Maven and Gradle.[2]

Using Maven

Maven is highly popular in the Java community. It allows you to describe the build process for your software together with its dependencies. In addition, there's a large community maintaining repositories that Maven can use to automatically download the libraries and dependencies used by your application. Maven was initially released in 2004 and as you might expect, XML was very popular back then! Consequently, the declaration of the build process in Maven is XML based.

Project structure

The great thing about Maven is that from the get-go it comes with structure to help maintenance. A Maven project starts with two main folders:

/src/main/java
: This is where you will develop and find all the Java classes required for your project.

src/test/java
: This where you will develop and find all the tests for your project.

There are two additional folders that are useful but not required:

src/main/resources
: This is where you can include extra resources such as text files needed by your application.

src/test/resources
: This is where you can include extra resources used by your tests.

Having this common directory layout allows anyone familiar with Maven to be immediately able to locate important files. To specify the build process you will need to create a *pom.xml* file where you specify various XML declarations to document the steps required to build your application. Figure 3-2 summarizes the common Maven project layout.

---

2 Earlier in Java's life there was another popular build tool, called Ant, but it is now considered end-of-life and should not be used anymore.

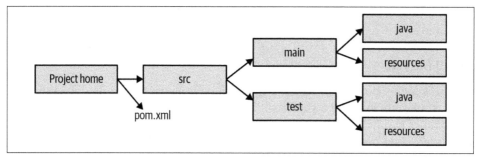

Figure 3-2. Maven standard directory layout

Example build file

The next step is to create the *pom.xml* that will dictate the build process. The code snippet in Example 3-26 shows a basic example that you can use for building the Bank Statements Analyzer project. You will see several elements in this file:

project
>   This is the top-level element in all *pom.xml* files.

groupId
>   This element indicates the unique identifier of the organization that created the project.

artifactId
>   This element specifies a unique base name for the artifact generated by the build process.

packaging
>   This element indicates the package type to be used by this artifact (e.g., JAR, WAR, EAR, etc.). The default is JAR if the XML element packaging is omitted.

version
>   The version of the artifact generated by the project.

build
>   This element specifies various configurations to guide the build process such as plug-ins and resources.

dependencies
>   This element specifies a dependency list for the project.

Example 3-26. Build file pom.xml in Maven

```xml
<?xml version="1.0" encoding="UTF-8"?>
<project xmlns="http://maven.apache.org/POM/4.0.0"
         xmlns:xsi="http://www.w3.org/2001/XMLSchema-instance"
         xsi:schemaLocation="http://maven.apache.org/POM/4.0.0 http://
maven.apache.org/xsd/maven-4.0.0.xsd">
    <modelVersion>4.0.0</modelVersion>

    <groupId>com.iteratrlearning</groupId>
    <artifactId>bankstatement_analyzer</artifactId>
    <version>1.0-SNAPSHOT</version>

    <build>
        <plugins>
            <plugin>
                <groupId>org.apache.maven.plugins</groupId>
                <artifactId>maven-compiler-plugin</artifactId>
                <version>3.7.0</version>
                <configuration>
                    <source>9</source>
                    <target>9</target>
                </configuration>
            </plugin>
        </plugins>
    </build>

    <dependencies>
        <dependency>
            <groupId>junit</groupId>
            <artifactId>junit</artifactId>
            <version>4.12</version>
            <scope>test</scope>
        </dependency>
    </dependenciesn>
</project>
```

Maven commands

Once you've set up a *pom.xml*, the next step is to use Maven to build and package your project! There are various commands available. We only cover the fundamentals:

`mvn clean`
    Cleans up any previously generated artifacts from a prior build

`mvn compile`
    Compiles the source code of the project (by default in a generated *target* folder)

```
mvn test
```
Tests the compiled source code

```
mvn package
```
Packages the compiled code in a suitable format such as JAR

For example, running the command `mvn package` from the directory where the *pom.xml* file is located will produce an output similar to this:

```
[INFO] Scanning for projects...
[INFO]
[INFO] -----------------------------------------------------------------------
[INFO] Building bankstatement_analyzer 1.0-SNAPSHOT
[INFO] -----------------------------------------------------------------------
[INFO]
[INFO] -----------------------------------------------------------------------
[INFO] BUILD SUCCESS
[INFO] -----------------------------------------------------------------------
[INFO] Total time: 1.063 s
[INFO] Finished at: 2018-06-10T12:14:48+01:00
[INFO] Final Memory: 10M/47M
```

You will see the generated JAR *bankstatement_analyzer-1.0-SNAPSHOT.jar* in the *target* folder.

> If you want to run a main class in the generated artifact using the `mvn` command, you will need to take a look at the exec plug-in (*https://oreil.ly/uoPbv*).

Using Gradle

Maven is not the only build tool solution available in the Java space. Gradle is an alternative popular build tool to Maven. But you may wonder why use yet another build tool? Isn't Maven the most widely adopted? One of Maven's deficiencies is that the use of XML can make things less readable and more cumbersome to work with. For example, it is often necessary as part of the build process to provide various custom system commands, such as copying and moving files around. Specifying such commands using an XML syntax isn't natural. In addition, XML is generally considered as a verbose language, which can increase the maintenance overhead. However, Maven introduced lots of good ideas such as standardization of project structure, which Gradle gets inspiration from. One of Gradle's biggest advantages is that it uses a friendly Domain Specific Language (DSL) using the Groovy or Kotlin programming languages to specify the build process. As a result, specifying the build is more natural, easier to customize, and simpler to understand. In addition, Gradle supports features such as cache and incremental compilation, which contribute to faster build time.[3]

Example build file

Gradle follows a similar project structure to Maven. However, instead of a *pom.xml* file, you will declare a *build.gradle* file. There's also a *settings.gradle* file that includes configuration variables and setup for a multiproject build. In the code snippet in Example 3-27 you can find a small build file written in Gradle that is equivalent to the Maven example you saw in Example 3-26. You have to admit it's a lot more concise!

Example 3-27. Build file build.gradle in Gradle

```
apply plugin: 'java'
apply plugin: 'application'

group = 'com.iteratrlearning'
version = '1.0-SNAPSHOT'

sourceCompatibility = 9
targetCompatibility = 9

mainClassName = "com.iteratrlearning.MainApplication"

repositories {
    mavenCentral()
}
dependencies {
    testImplementation group: 'junit', name: 'junit', version:'4.12'
}
```

Gradle commands

Finally, you can now run the build process by running similar commands to what you learned with Maven. Each command in Gradle is a task. You can define your own tasks and execute them or use built-in tasks such as test, build, and clean:

gradle clean
: Cleans up generated files during a previous build

gradle build
: Packages the application

gradle test
: Runs the tests

---

3 For more information on Maven versus Gradle, see *https://gradle.org/maven-vs-gradle/*.

```
gradle run
```
Runs the main class specified in `mainClassName` provided the `application` plug-in is applied

For example, running `gradle build` will produce an output similar to this:

```
BUILD SUCCESSFUL in 1s
2 actionable tasks: 2 executed
```

You will find the generated JAR in the `build` folder that is created by Gradle during the build process.

Takeaways

- The Open/Closed Principle promotes the idea of being able to change the behavior of a method or class without having to modify the code.
- The Open/Closed Principle reduces fragility of code by not changing existing code, promotes reusability of existing code, and promotes decoupling, which leads to better code maintenance.
- God interfaces with many specific methods introduce complexity and coupling.
- An interface that is too granular with single methods can introduce the opposite of cohesion.
- You should not be worried about adding descriptive method names to help readability and comprehension of your API .
- Returning `void` as a result of an operation makes it difficult to test its behavior.
- Exceptions in Java contribute to documentation, type safety, and separation of concerns.
- Use checked exceptions sparingly rather than the default as they can cause significant clutter.
- Overly specific exceptions can make software development unproductive.
- The Notification Pattern introduces a domain class to collect errors.
- Do not ignore an exception or catch the generic `Exception` as you will lose the benefits of diagnosing the root of the problem.
- A build tool automates the repetitive tasks in the software development life cycle including building, testing, and deploying your application.
- Maven and Gradle are two popular build tools used in the Java community.

Iterating on You

If you want to extend and solidify the knowledge from this section you could try one of these activities:

- Add support for exporting in different data formats including JSON and XML
- Develop a basic GUI around the Bank Statements Analyzer

Completing the Challenge

Mark Erbergzuck is very happy with your final iteration of the Bank Statements Analyzer. A few days later, the world hit a new financial crisis and your application is going viral. Time to work on a new exciting project in the next chapter!

CHAPTER 4

The Document Management System

The Challenge

After successfully implementing an advanced Bank Statements Analyzer for Mark Erbergzuck you decide to run some errands—including going to an appointment with your dentist. Dr. Avaj has run her practice successfully for many years. Her happy patients retain their white teeth well into old age. The downside of such a successful practice is that every year more and more patient documents get generated. Every time she needs to find a record of prior treatment, her assistants spend longer and longer searching their filing cabinets.

She realizes that it's time to automate the process of managing these documents and keeping track of them. Luckily, she has a patient who can do that for her! You are going to help by writing software for her that manages these documents and enables her to find the information that will allow her practice to thrive and grow.

The Goal

In this chapter you'll be learning about a variety of different software development principles. Key to the design of managing documents is an inheritance relationship, which means extending a class or implementing an interface. In order to do this the right way you'll get to understand the Liskov Substitution Principle, named after famed computer scientist Barbara Liskov.

Your understanding of when to use inheritance will get fleshed out with a discussion of the "Composition over Inheritance" principle.

Finally, you'll extend your knowledge of how to write automated test code by understanding what makes a good and maintainable test. Now that we've spoiled the plot of this chapter, let's get back to understanding what requirements Dr. Avaj has for the Document Management System.

 If at any point you want to look at the source code for this chapter, you can look at the package com.iteratrlearning.shu_book.chapter_04 in the book's code repository.

Document Management System Requirements

A friendly cup of tea with Dr. Avaj has revealed that she has the documents that she wants to manage as files on her computer. The Document Management System needs to be able to import these files and record some information about each file that can be indexed and searched. There are three types of documents that she cares about:

Reports
> A body of text detailing some consultation of operation on a patient.

Letters
> A text document that gets sent to an address. (You're probably familiar with these already, come to think of it.)

Images
> The dental practice often records x-rays or photos of teeth and gums. These have a size.

In addition, all documents need to record the path to the file that is being managed and what patient the document is about. Dr. Avaj needs to be able to search these documents, and query whether each of the attributes about a different type of document contains certain pieces of information; for example, to search for letters where the body contains "Joe Bloggs."

During the conversation, you also established that Dr. Avaj might wish to add other types of documents in the future.

Fleshing Out the Design

When approaching this problem, there are lots of big design choices to make and modeling approaches that we could take. These choices are subjective, and you're welcome to try to code up a solution to Dr. Avaj's problem before or after reading this chapter. In "Alternative Approaches" on page 73 you can see the reasons why we avoid different choices and the overarching principles behind them.

One good first step to approaching any program is to start with test-driven development (TDD), which is what we did when writing the book's sample solution. We won't be covering TDD until Chapter 5, so let's begin with thinking about the behaviors that your software needs to perform and incrementally fleshing out the code that implements these behaviors.

The Document Management System should be able to import documents on request and add them into its internal store of documents. In order to fulfill this requirement, let's create the `DocumentManagementSystem` class and add two methods:

`void importFile(String path)`
> Takes a path to a file that our user wants to import to the Document Management System. As this is a public API method that might take input from users in a production system, we take our path as a `String` rather than relying on a more type-safe class like `java.nio.Path` or `java.io.File`.

`List<Document> contents()`
> Returns a list of all the documents that the Document Management System currently stores.

You'll notice that `contents()` returns a list of some `Document` class. We've not said what this class entails yet, but it'll reappear in due course. For now, you can pretend that it's an empty class.

Importers

A key characteristic of this system is that we need to be able to import documents of different types. For the purposes of this system you can rely on the files' extensions in order to decide how to import them, since Dr. Avaj has been saving files with very specific extensions. All her letters have the *.letter* extension, reports have *.report*, and *.jpg* is the only image format used.

The simplest thing to do would be to just throw all the code for the importing mechanism into a single method, as shown in Example 4-1.

Example 4-1. Switch of extension example

```
switch(extension) {
    case "letter":
        // code for importing letters.
        break;

    case "report":
        // code for importing reports.
        break;
```

```
    case "jpg":
        // code for importing images.
        break;

    default:
        throw new UnknownFileTypeException("For file: " + path);
}
```

This approach would have solved the problem in question but would be hard to extend. Every time you want to add another type of file that gets processed you would need to implement another entry in the switch statement. Over time this method would become intractably long and hard to read.

If you keep your main class nice and simple and split out different implementation classes for importing different types of documents, then it's easy to locate and understand each importer in isolation. In order to support different document types, an Importer interface is defined. Each Importer will be a class that can import a different type of file.

Now that we know we need an interface to import the files, how should we represent the file that is going to be imported? We have a couple of different options: use a plain String to represent the path of the file, or use a class that represents a file, like java.io.File.

You could make the case that we should apply the principle of strong typing here: take a type that represents the file and reduce the scope for errors versus using a String. Let's take that approach and use a java.io.File object as the parameter in our Importer interface to represent the file being imported, as shown in Example 4-2.

Example 4-2. Importer

```
interface Importer {
    Document importFile(File file) throws IOException;
}
```

You might be asking, *Why don't you use a File for the public API of DocumentManage mentSystem as well then?* Well, in the case of this application, our public API would probably be wrapped up in some kind of user interface, and we aren't sure what form that is taking files in. As a result we kept things simple and just used a String type.

The Document Class

Let's also define the Document class at this point in time. Each document will have multiple attributes that we can search on. Different documents have different types of attributes. We have several different options that we can consider the pros and cons of when defining the Document.

The first and simplest way to represent a document would be to use a `Map<String, String>`, which is a map from attribute names to values associated with those attributes. So why not just pass a `Map<String, String>` around through the application? Well, introducing a domain class to model a single document is not just drinking the OOP Koolaid, but also provides a series of practical improvements in application maintability and readability.

For a start, the value of giving concrete names to components within an application cannot be overstated. Communication is King! Good teams of software developers use a *Ubiquitous Language* to describe their software. Matching the vocabulary that you use within the code of your application to the vocabulary that you use to talk to clients like Dr. Avaj makes things a lot easier to maintain. When you have a conversation with a colleague or client you will invariably need to agree upon some common language with which to describe different aspects of the software. By mapping this to the code itself, it makes it really easy to know what part of the code to change. This is called *discoverability*.

 The term *Ubiquitous Language* was coined by Eric Evans and originates in *Domain Driven Design*. It refers to the use of a common language that is clearly degined and shared between both developers and users.

Another principle that should encourage you to introduce a class to model a document is strong typing. Many people use this term to refer to the nature of a programming language, but here we're talking about the more practical use of strong typing in implementing your software. Types allow us to restrict the way in which data is used. For example, our `Document` class is immutable: once it has been created you can't change, or *mutate*, any of its attributes. Our `Importer` implementations create the documents; nothing else modifies them. If you ever see a `Document` with an error in one of its attributes, you can narrow the source of the bug down to the specific `Importer` that created the `Document`. You can also infer from the immutability that it's possible to index or cache any information associated with the `Document` and you know that it will be correct forever, since documents are immutable.

Another design choice that developers might consider when modeling their `Document` would be make the `Document` extend `HashMap<String, String>`. At first that seems great because the `HashMap` has all the functionality you need to model a `Document`. However, there are several reasons why this is a bad choice.

Software design is often as much about restricting functionality that is undesirable as it is about building things that you do want. We would have instantly thrown away the aforementioned benefits from immutability by allowing anything in the application to modify the `Document` class if it were just a subclass of `HashMap`. Wrapping the collection also gives us an opportunity to give more meaningful names to the methods, instead of, for example, looking up an attribute by calling the `get()` method, which doesn't really mean anything! Later on we'll go into more detail about inheritance versus composition, because this is really a specific example of that discussion.

In short, domain classes allow us to name a concept and restrict the possible behaviors and values of this concept in order to improve discoverability and reduce the scope for bugs. As a result, we've chosen to model the `Document` as shown in Example 4-3. If you're wondering why it isn't `public` like most interfaces, this is discussed later in "Scoping and Encapsulation Choices" on page 73.

Example 4-3. Document

```java
public class Document {
    private final Map<String, String> attributes;

    Document(final Map<String, String> attributes) {
        this.attributes = attributes;
    }

    public String getAttribute(final String attributeName) {
        return attributes.get(attributeName);
    }
}
```

One final thing to note about `Document` is that it has a package-scoped constructor. Often Java classes make their constructor `public`, but this can be a bad choice as it allows code anywhere in your project to create objects of that type. Only code in the Document Management System should be able to create `Documents`, so we keep the constructor package scoped and restrict access to only the package that the Document Management System lives in.

Attributes and Hierarchical Documents

In our `Document` class we used `Strings` for attributes. Doesn't this go against the principle of strong typing? The answer here is yes and no. We are storing attributes as text so that they can be searched through a text-based search. Not only that, but we want to ensure that all attributes are created in a very generic form that is independent of the `Importer` that created them. `Strings` aren't a bad choice as such in this context. It should be noted that passing `Strings` around throughout an application in order to represent information is often considered a bad idea. In contrast with something being strongly typed, this is termed stringly typed!

In particular, if more complicated use was being made of the attribute values, then having different attribute types parsed out would be useful. For example, if we wanted to be able to find addresses within a certain distance or images with a height and width less than a certain size, then having strongly typed attributes would be a boon. It would be a lot easier to make comparisons with a width value that is an integer. In the case of this Document Management System, however, we simply don't need that functionality.

You could design the Document Management System with a class hierarchy for Docu ments that models the Importer hierarchy. For example, a ReportImporter imports instances of the Report class that extends the Document class. This passes our basic sanity check for subclassing. In other words, it allows you to say a Report is a Docu ment and it makes sense as a sentence. We chose not to go down that direction, how ever, as the right way to model classes in an OOP setting is to think in terms of behavior and data.

The documents are all modeled very generically in terms of named attributes, rather than specific fields that exist within different subclasses. Additionally, as far as this system is concerned, documents have very little behavior associated with them. There was simply no point in adding a class hierarchy here when it provided no benefit. You might think that this statement in and of itself is a little arbitrary, but it informs us of another principle: KISS.

You learned about the KISS principle in Chapter 2. KISS means that designs are better if they are kept simple. It's often very hard to avoid unnecessary complexity, but it's worth trying hard to do so. Whenever someone says, "we might need X" or "it would be cool if we also did Y," just say No. Bloated and complex designs are paved with good intentions around extensibility and code that is a nice-to-have rather than must-have.

Implementing and Registering Importers

You can implement the Importer interface to look up different types of files. Example 4-4 shows the way that images are imported. One of the great things about Java's core library is that it provides a lot of built-in functionality right out of the box. Here we read an image file using the ImageIO.read method and then extract the width and height of the image from the resulting BufferedImage object.

Example 4-4. ImageImporter

```
import static com.iteratrlearning.shu_book.chapter_04.Attributes.*;

class ImageImporter implements Importer {
    @Override
    public Document importFile(final File file) throws IOException {
        final Map<String, String> attributes = new HashMap<>();
        attributes.put(PATH, file.getPath());

        final BufferedImage image = ImageIO.read(file);
```

```
        attributes.put(WIDTH, String.valueOf(image.getWidth()));
        attributes.put(HEIGHT, String.valueOf(image.getHeight()));
        attributes.put(TYPE, "IMAGE");

        return new Document(attributes);
    }
}
```

Attribute names are constants defined in the `Attributes` class. This avoids bugs where different importers end up using different strings for the same attribute name; for example, `"Path"` versus `"path"`. Java itself doesn't have a direct concept of a constant as such, Example 4-5 shows the commonly used idiom. This constant is `public` because we want to be able to use it from different importers, though you may well have a `private` or `package` scoped constant instead. The use of the `final` keyword ensures that it can't be reassigned to and `static` ensures that there is only a single instance per class.

Example 4-5. How to define a constant in Java

```
public static final String PATH = "path";
```

There are importers for all three different types of files and you will see the other two implemented in "Extending and Reusing Code" on page 74. Don't worry, we're not hiding anything up our sleeves. In order to be able to use the `Importer` classes when we import files, we also need to register the importers to look them up. We use the extension of the file that we want to import as the key of the `Map`, as shown in Example 4-6.

Example 4-6. Registering the importers

```
    private final Map<String, Importer> extensionToImporter = new HashMap<>();

    public DocumentManagementSystem() {
        extensionToImporter.put("letter", new LetterImporter());
        extensionToImporter.put("report", new ReportImporter());
        extensionToImporter.put("jpg", new ImageImporter());
    }
```

Now that you know how to import documents, we can implement search. We won't be focusing on the most efficient way to implement searching of documents here since we're not trying to implement Google, just get the information to Dr. Avaj that she requires. A conversation with Dr. Avaj revealed that she wanted to be able to look up information about different attributes of a `Document`.

Her requirements could be met by just being able to find subsequences within attribute values. For example, she might want to search for documents that have a patient called Joe, and with *Diet Coke* in the body. We thus devised a very simple query language that consisted of a series of attribute name and substring pairs separated by commas. Our aforementioned query would be written as `"patient:Joe,body:Diet Coke"`.

Since the search implementation keeps things simple rather than trying to be highly optimized, it just does a linear scan over all the documents recorded in the system and tests each one against the query. The query `String` that is passed to the `search` method is parsed into a `Query` object that can then be tested against each `Document`.

The Liskov Substitution Principle (LSP)

We've talked about a few specific design decisions related to classes—for example, modeling different `Importer` implementations with classes, and why we didn't introduce a class hierarchy for the `Document` class and why we didn't just make `Document` extend `HashMap`. But really there's a broader principle at stake here, one that allows us to generalize these examples into an approach that you can use in any piece of software. This is called the *Liskov Substitution Principle* (LSP) and it helps us understand how to subclass and implement interfaces correctly. LSP forms the L of the SOLID principles that we've been referring to throughout this book.

The Liskov Substitution Principle is often stated in these very formal terms, but is actually a very simple concept. Let's demystify some of this terminology. If you hear *type* in this context, just think of a class or an interface. The term *subtype* means establish a parent-to-child relationship between types; in other words, extend a class or implement an interface. So informally you can think of this as meaning that child classes should maintain the behavior they inherit from their parents. We know, we know—it sounds like an obvious statement, but we can be more specific and split out LSP into four distinct parts:

LSP

Let $q(x)$ be a property provable about objects x of type T. Then $q(y)$ should be true for objects y of type S where S is a subtype of T.

Preconditions cannot be strengthened in a subtype

A precondition establishes the conditions under which some code will work. You can't just assume what you've written will work anyway, anyhow, anywhere. For example, all our `Importer` implementations have the precondition that the file being imported exists and is readable. As a result, the `importFile` method has validation code before any `Importer` is invoked, as can be seen in Example 4-7.

Example 4-7. importFile definition

```java
public void importFile(final String path) throws IOException {
    final File file = new File(path);
    if (!file.exists()) {
        throw new FileNotFoundException(path);
    }

    final int separatorIndex = path.lastIndexOf('.');
    if (separatorIndex != -1) {
        if (separatorIndex == path.length()) {
            throw new UnknownFileTypeException("No extension found For
file: " + path);
        }
        final String extension = path.substring(separatorIndex + 1);
        final Importer importer = extensionToImporter.get(extension);
        if (importer == null) {
            throw new UnknownFileTypeException("For file: " + path);
        }

        final Document document = importer.importFile(file);
        documents.add(document);
    } else {
        throw new UnknownFileTypeException("No extension found For
file: " + path);
    }
}
```

LSP means that you can't require any more restrictive preconditions than your parent required. So, for example, you can't require your document to be smaller than 100KB in size if your parent should be able to import any size of document.

Postconditions cannot be weakened in a subtype

This might sound a bit confusing because it reads a lot like the first rule. Postconditions are things that have to be true after some code has run. For example, after importFile() has run, if the file in question is valid it must be in the list of documents returned by contents(). So if the parent has some kind of side effect or returns some value, then the child must do so as well.

Invariants of the supertype must be preserved in a subtype

An invariant is something that never changes, like the ebb and flow of the tides. In the context of inheritance, we want to make sure that any invariants that are expected to be maintained by the parent class should also be maintained by the children.

The History Rule

This is the hardest aspect of LSP to understand. In essence, the child class shouldn't allow state changes that your parent disallowed. So, in our example program we have an immutable Document class. In other words, once it has been instantiated you can't remove, add, or alter any of the attributes. You shouldn't subclass this Document class and create a mutable Document class. This is because any user of the parent class would expect certain behavior in response to calling methods on the Document class. If the child were mutable, it could violate callers' expectations about what calling those methods does.

Alternative Approaches

You could have taken a completely different approach when it comes to designing the Document Management System. We'll take a look at some of these alternatives now as we think they are instructive. None of the choices could be considered wrong as such, but we do think the chosen approach is best.

Making Importer a Class

You could have chosen to make a class hierarchy for importers, and have a class at the top for the Importer rather than an interface. Interfaces and classes provide a different set of capabilities. You can implement multiple interfaces, while classes can contain instance fields and it's more usual to have method bodies in classes.

In this case the reason to have a hierarchy is to enable different importers to be used. You've already heard about our motivation for avoiding brittle class-based inheritance relationships, so it should be pretty clear that using interfaces is a better choice here.

That's not to say that classes wouldn't be a better choice elsewhere. If you want to model a strong *is a* relationship in your problem domain that involves state or a lot of behavior, then class-based inheritance is more appropriate. It's just not the choice we think is most appropriate here.

Scoping and Encapsulation Choices

If you have taken the time to peruse the code you might notice that the Importer interface, its implementations, and our Query class are all package scoped. Package scope is the default scope, so if you see a class file with class Query at the top you know it's package scoped, and if it says public class Query it's public scoped. Package scoping means that other classes within the same package can *see* or *have access* to the class, but no one else can. It's a cloaking device.

A strange thing about the Java ecosystem is that even though package scope is the default scope, whenever we've been involved in software development projects there are always more public-scoped classes than package-scoped ones. Perhaps the default should have been public all along, but either way package scope is a really useful tool. It helps you encapsulate these kinds of design decisions. A lot of this section has commented on the different choices that are available to you around designing the system, and you may want to refactor to one of these alternative designs when maintaining the system. This would be harder if we leaked details about this implementation outside of the package in question. Through diligent use of package scoping you can stop classes outside of the package making so many assumptions about that internal design.

We think it's also worth reiterating that this is simply a justification and explanation of these design choices. There's nothing inherently wrong with making other choices listed in this section—they may work out to be more appropriate depending on how the application evolves over time.

Extending and Reusing Code

When it comes to software, the only constant is change. Over time you may want to add features to your product, customer requirements may change, and regulations could force you alter your software. As we alluded to earlier, there may be more documents that Dr. Avaj would like to add to our Document Management System. In fact, when we first came to showcase the software that we've written for her she immediately realized that invoicing clients was something that she also wanted to keep track of in this system. An invoice is a document with a body and an amount and has an *.invoice* extension. Example 4-8 shows an example invoice.

Example 4-8. Invoice example

```
Dear Joe Bloggs

Here is your invoice for the dental treatment that you received.

Amount: $100

regards,

  Dr Avaj
  Awesome Dentist
```

Fortunately for us, all of Dr. Avaj's invoices are in the same format. As you can see, we need to extract an amount of money from this, and the amount line starts with the `Amount:` prefix. The person's name is at the beginning of the letter on a line with the prefix `Dear`. In fact, our system implements a general method of finding the suffix of a line with a given prefix, shown in Example 4-9. In this example, the field `lines` has already been initialized with the lines of the file that we're importing. We pass this method a `prefix`—for example, "Amount:"—and it associates the rest of the line, the suffix, with a provided attribute name.

Example 4-9. addLineSuffix definition

```
void addLineSuffix(final String prefix, final String attributeName) {
    for(final String line: lines) {
        if (line.startsWith(prefix)) {
            attributes.put(attributeName, line.substring(prefix.length()));
            break;
        }
    }
}
```

We in fact have a similar concept when we try to import a letter. Consider the example letter presented in Example 4-10. Here you can extract the name of the patient by looking for a line starting with `Dear`. Letters also have addresses and bodies of text that you want to extract from the contents of the text file.

Example 4-10. Letter example

```
Dear Joe Bloggs

123 Fake Street
Westminster
London
United Kingdom

We are writing to you to confirm the re-scheduling of your appointment
with Dr. Avaj from 29th December 2016 to 5th January 2017.

regards,

  Dr Avaj
  Awesome Dentist
```

We also have a similar problem when it comes to importing patient reports. Dr. Avaj's reports prefix the name of the patient with `Patient:` and have a body of text to include, just like letters. You can see an example of a report in Example 4-11.

Example 4-11. Report example

```
Patient: Joe Bloggs

On 5th January 2017 I examined Joe's teeth.
We discussed his switch from drinking Coke to Diet Coke.
No new problems were noted with his teeth.
```

So one option here would be to have all three text-based importers implement the same method to find the suffixes of text lines with a given prefix that was listed in Example 4-9. Now if we were charging Dr. Avaj based on the number of lines of code that we had written, this would be a great strategy. We could triple the amount of money that we would make for basically the same work!

Sadly (or maybe not so sadly, given the aforementioned incentives), customers rarely pay based on the number of lines of code produced. What matters are the requirements that the customer wants. So we really want to be able to reuse this code across the three importers. In order to reuse the code we need to actually have it live in some class. You have essentially three options to consider, each with pros and cons:

- Use a *utility* class
- Use *inheritance*
- Use a domain class

The simplest option to start with is to create a utility class. You could call this `ImportU til`. Then every time you wanted to have a method that needs to be shared between different importers it could go in this utility class. Your utility class would end up being a bag of static methods.

While a utility class is nice and simple, it's not exactly the pinnacle of object-oriented programming. The object-oriented style involves having concepts in your application be modeled by classes. If you want to create a thing, then you invoke `new Thing()` for whatever your thing is. Attributes and behavior associated with the thing should be methods on the `Thing` class.

If you follow this principle of modeling real-world objects as classes, it does genuinely make it easier to understand your application because it gives you a structure and maps a mental model of your domain onto your code. You want to alter the way that letters are imported? Well then edit the `LetterImporter` class.

Utility classes violate this expectation and often end up turning into bundles of procedural code with no single responsibility or concept. Over time, this can often lead to the appearance of a God Class in our codebase; in other words, a single large class that ends up hogging a lot of responsibility.

So what should you do if you want to associate this behavior to a concept? Well, the next most obvious approach might be to use inheritance. In this approach you would have the different importers extend a `TextImporter` class. You could then place all the common functionality on that class and reuse it in subclasses.

Inheritance is a perfectly solid choice of design in many circumstances. You've already seen the Liskov Substitution Principle and how it puts constraints on the correctness of our inheritance relationship. In practice, inheritance is often a poor choice when the inheritance fails to model some real-world relationship.

In this case, a `TextImporter` is an `Importer` and we can ensure that our classes follow the LSP rules, but it doesn't really seem like a strong concept to work with. The issue with inheritance relationships that don't correspond to real-world relationships is that they tend to be brittle. As your application evolves over time you want abstractions that evolve with the application rather than against it. As a rule of thumb, it's a bad idea to introduce an inheritance relationship purely to enable code reuse.

Our final choice is to model the text file using a domain class. To use this approach we would model some underlying concept and build out our different importers by invoking methods on top of the underlying concept. So what's the concept in question here? Well, what we're really trying to do is manipulate the contents of a text file, so let's call the class a `TextFile`. It's not original or creative, but that's the point. You know where the functionality for manipulating text files lies, because the class is named in a really dead simple manner.

Example 4-12 shows the definition of the class and its fields. Note that this isn't a subclass of a `Document` because a document shouldn't be coupled to just text files—we may import binary files like images as well. This is just a class that models the underlying concept of a text file and has associated methods for extracting data from text files.

Example 4-12. TextFile definition

```
class TextFile {
    private final Map<String, String> attributes;
    private final List<String> lines;

    // class continues ...
```

This is the approach that we pick in the case of importers. We think this allows us to model our problem domain in a flexible way. It doesn't tie us into a brittle inheritance hierarchy, but still allows us to reuse the code. Example 4-13 shows how to import invoices. The suffixes for the name and amount are added, along with setting the type of the invoice to be an amount.

Example 4-13. Importing invoices

```
    @Override
    public Document importFile(final File file) throws IOException {
        final TextFile textFile = new TextFile(file);

        textFile.addLineSuffix(NAME_PREFIX, PATIENT);
        textFile.addLineSuffix(AMOUNT_PREFIX, AMOUNT);

        final Map<String, String> attributes = textFile.getAttributes();
        attributes.put(TYPE, "INVOICE");
```

```
        return new Document(attributes);
    }
```

You can also see another example of an importer that uses the `TextFile` class in
Example 4-14. No need to worry about how `TextFile.addLines` is implemented; you
can see an explanation of that in Example 4-15.

Example 4-14. Importing letters

```
    @Override
    public Document importFile(final File file) throws IOException {
        final TextFile textFile = new TextFile(file);

        textFile.addLineSuffix(NAME_PREFIX, PATIENT);

        final int lineNumber = textFile.addLines(2, String::isEmpty, ADDRESS);
        textFile.addLines(lineNumber + 1, (line) -> line.startsWith("regards,"),
BODY);

        final Map<String, String> attributes = textFile.getAttributes();
        attributes.put(TYPE, "LETTER");
        return new Document(attributes);
    }
```

These classes weren't first written like this, though. They evolved into their current
state. When we started coding up the Document Management System, the first text-
based importer, the `LetterImporter`, had all of its text extraction logic written inline
in the class. This is a good way to start. Trying to seek out code to reuse often results
in inappropriate abstractions. Walk before you run.

As we started writing the `ReportImporter` it become increasingly apparent that a lot
of the text extraction logic could be shared between the two importers, and that really
they should be written in terms of method invocations upon some common domain
concept that we have introduced here—the `TextFile`. In fact, we even copy and pas-
ted the code that was to be shared between the two classes to begin with.

That isn't to say that copy and pasting code is good—far from it. But it's often better
to duplicate a little bit of code when you start writing some classes. Once you've
implemented more of the application, the right abstraction—e.g., a `TextFile` class
will become apparent. Only when you know a little bit more about the right way to
remove duplication should you go down the route of removing the duplication.

In Example 4-15 you can see how the `TextFile.addLines` method was implemented.
This is common code used by different `Importer` implementations. Its first argument
is a `start` index, which tells you which line number to start on. Then there's an `isEnd`
predicate that is applied to the line and returns `true` if we've reached the end of the

line. Finally, we have the name of the attribute that we're going to associate with this value.

Example 4-15. addLines definition

```
int addLines(
    final int start,
    final Predicate<String> isEnd,
    final String attributeName) {

    final StringBuilder accumulator = new StringBuilder();
    int lineNumber;
    for (lineNumber = start; lineNumber < lines.size(); lineNumber++) {
        final String line = lines.get(lineNumber);
        if (isEnd.test(line)) {
            break;
        }

        accumulator.append(line);
        accumulator.append("\n");
    }
    attributes.put(attributeName, accumulator.toString().trim());
    return lineNumber;
}
```

Test Hygiene

As you learned in Chapter 2, writing automated tests has a lot of benefits in terms of software maintainability. It enables us to reduce the scope for regressions and understand which commit caused them. It also enables us to refactor our code with confidence. Tests aren't a magic panacea, though. They require that we write and maintain a lot of code in order to get these benefits. As you know, writing and maintaining code is a difficult proposition, and many developers find that when they first start writing automated tests that they can take a lot of developer time.

In order to solve the problem of test maintainability you need to get to grips with *test hygiene*. Test hygiene means to keep your test code clean and ensure that it is maintained and improved along with your codebase under test. If you don't maintain and treat your tests, over time they will become a burden on your developer productivity. In this section you'll learn about a few key points that can help to keep tests hygienic.

Test Naming

The first thing to think about when it comes to tests is their naming. Developers can get highly opinionated about naming—it's an easy topic to talk about a lot because everyone can relate to it and think about the problem. We think the thing to remember is that there's rarely a clear, really good name for something, but there are many, many, bad names.

The first test we wrote for the Document Management System was testing that we import a file and create a `Document`. This was written before we had introduced the concept of an `Importer` and weren't testing `Document`-specific attributes. The code is in Example 4-16.

Example 4-16. Test for importing files

```
@Test
public void shouldImportFile() throws Exception
{
    system.importFile(LETTER);

    final Document document = onlyDocument();

    assertAttributeEquals(document, Attributes.PATH, LETTER);
}
```

This test was named `shouldImportFile`. The key driving principles when it comes to test naming are readability, maintainability, and acting as *executable documentation*. When you see a report of a test class being run, the names should act as statements that document what functionality works and what does not. This allows a developer to easily map from application behavior to a test that asserts that this behavior is implemented. By reducing the impedance mismatch between behavior and code, we make it easier for other developers to understand what is happening in the future. This is a test that confirms that the document management system imports a file.

There are lots of naming anti-patterns, however. The worst anti-pattern is to name a test something completely nondescript—for example, `test1`. What on earth is `test1` testing? The reader's patience? Treat people who are reading your code like you would like them to treat you.

Another common test naming anti-pattern is just named after a concept or a noun—for example, `file` or `document`. Test names should describe the behavior under test, not a concept. Another test naming anti-pattern is to simply name the test after a method that is invoked during testing, rather than the behavior. In this case the test might be named `importFile`.

You might ask, by naming our test `shouldImportFile` haven't we committed this sin here? There's some merit to the accusation, but here we're just describing the behavior under test. In fact, the `importFile` method is tested by various tests; for example, `shouldImportLetterAttributes`, `shouldImportReportAttributes`, and `shouldImportImageAttributes`. None of those tests are called `importFile`—they are all describing more specific behaviors.

OK, now you know what bad naming looks like, so what is good test naming? You should follow three rules of thumb and use them to drive test naming:

Use domain terminology
Align the vocabulary used in your test names with that used when describing the problem domain or referred by the application itself.

Use natural language
Every test name should be something that you can easily read as a sentence. It should always describe some behavior in a readable way.

Be descriptive
Code will be read many times more often than it is written. Don't skimp on spending more time thinking of a good name that's descriptive up front and easier to understand later down the line. If you can't think of a good name, why not ask a colleague? In golf, you win by putting in the fewest shots. Programming isn't like that; shortest isn't necessarily best.

You can follow the convention used in the `DocumentManagementSystemTest` of prefixing test names with the word "should," or choose not to; that's merely a matter of personal preference.

Behavior Not Implementation

If you're writing a test for a class, a component, or even a system, then you should only be testing the *public behavior* of whatever is being tested. In the case of the Document Management System, we only have tests for the behavior of our public API in the form of `DocumentManagementSystemTest`. In this test we test the public API of the `DocumentManagementSystem` class and thus the whole system. The API can be seen in Example 4-17.

Example 4-17. Public API of the DocumentManagementSystem class

```
public class DocumentManagementSystem
{
    public void importFile(final String path) {
        ...
    }

    public List<Document> contents() {
        ...
    }

    public List<Document> search(final String query) {
        ...
    }
}
```

Our tests should only invoke these public API methods and not try to inspect the internal state of the objects or the design. This is one of the key mistakes made by developers that leads to hard-to-maintain tests. Relying on specific implementation details results in brittle tests because if you change the implementation detail in question, the test can start to fail even if the behavior is still working. Take a look at the test in Example 4-18.

Example 4-18. Test for importing letters

```
@Test
public void shouldImportLetterAttributes() throws Exception
{
    system.importFile(LETTER);

    final Document document = onlyDocument();

    assertAttributeEquals(document, PATIENT, JOE_BLOGGS);
    assertAttributeEquals(document, ADDRESS,
        "123 Fake Street\n" +
            "Westminster\n" +
            "London\n" +
            "United Kingdom");
    assertAttributeEquals(document, BODY,
        "We are writing to you to confirm the re-scheduling of your appointment
\n" +
        "with Dr. Avaj from 29th December 2016 to 5th January 2017.");
    assertTypeIs("LETTER", document);
}
```

One way of testing this letter-importing functionality would have been to write the test as a unit test on the `LetterImporter` class. This would have looked fairly similar: importing an example file and then making an assert about the result returned from the importer. In our tests, though, the mere existence of the `LetterImporter` is an implementation detail. In "Extending and Reusing Code" on page 74, you saw numerous other alternative choices for laying out our importer code. By laying out our tests in this manner, we give ourselves the choice to refactor our internals to a different design without breaking our tests.

So we've said that relying on the behavior of a class relies on using the public API, but there's also some parts of the behavior that aren't usually restricted just through making methods public or private. For example, we might not want to rely on the order of documents being being returned from the `contents()` method. That isn't a property that's restricted by the public API of the `DocumentManagementSystem` class, but simply something that you need to be careful to avoid doing.

A common anti-pattern in this regard is exposing otherwise private state through a getter or setter in order to make testing easier. You should try to avoid doing this wherever possible as it makes your tests brittle. If you have exposed this state to make testing superficially easier, then you end up making maintaining your application harder in the long run. This is because any change to your codebase that involves changing the way this internal state is represented now also requires altering your tests. This is sometimes a good indication that you need to refactor out a new class that can be more easily and effectively tested.

Don't Repeat Yourself

"Extending and Reusing Code" on page 74 extensively discusses how we can remove duplicate code from our application and where to place the resulting code. The exact same reasoning around maintenance applies equally to test code. Sadly, developers often simply don't bother to remove duplication from tests in the same way as they would for application code. If you take a look at Example 4-19 you'll see a test that repeatedly makes asserts about the different attributes that a resulting Document has.

Example 4-19. Test for importing images

```
@Test
public void shouldImportImageAttributes() throws Exception
{
    system.importFile(XRAY);

    final Document document = onlyDocument();

    assertAttributeEquals(document, WIDTH, "320");
    assertAttributeEquals(document, HEIGHT, "179");
    assertTypeIs("IMAGE", document);
}
```

Normally you would have to look up the attribute name for every attribute and assert that it is equal to an expected value. In the case of the tests here, this is a common enough operation that a common method, assertAttributeEquals, was extracted with this logic. Its implementation is shown in Example 4-20.

Example 4-20. Implementing a new assertion

```
private void assertAttributeEquals(
    final Document document,
    final String attributeName,
    final String expectedValue)
{
    assertEquals(
        "Document has the wrong value for " + attributeName,
        expectedValue,
        document.getAttribute(attributeName));
}
```

Good Diagnostics

Tests would be no good if they didn't fail. In fact, if you've never seen a test fail how do you know if it's working at all? When writing tests the best thing to do is to optimize for failure. When we say optimize, we don't mean make the test run faster when it fails—we mean ensure that it is written in a way that makes understanding why and how it failed as easy as possible. The trick to this is good *diagnostics*.

By diagnostics we mean the message and information that gets printed out when a test fails. The clearer this message is about what has failed, the easier it is to debug the test failure. You might ask why even bother with this when a lot of the time Java tests are run from within modern IDEs that have debuggers built in? Well, sometimes tests may be run within continuous integration environments, and sometimes they may be from the command line. Even if you're running them within an IDE it is still helpful to have good diagnostic information. Hopefully, we've convinced you of the need for good diagnostics, but what do they look like in code?

Example 4-21 shows a method that asserts that the system only contains a single document. We will explain the `hasSize()` method in a little bit.

Example 4-21. Test that the system contains a single document

```
private Document onlyDocument()
{
    final List<Document> documents = system.contents();
    assertThat(documents, hasSize(1));
    return documents.get(0);
}
```

The simplest type of assert that JUnit offers us is `assertTrue()`, which will take a boolean value that it expects to be true. Example 4-22 shows how we could have just used `assertTrue` to implement the test. In this case the value is being checked to equal 0 so that it will fail the `shouldImportFile` test and thus demonstrate the failure diagnostics. The problem with this is that we don't get very good diagnostics—just an `AssertionError` with no information in the message shown in Figure 4-1. You don't know what failed, and you don't know what values were being compared. You know nothing, even if your name isn't Jon Snow.

Example 4-22. assertTrue example

```
assertTrue(documents.size() == 0);
```

Figure 4-1. Screenshot of assertTrue failing

The most commonly used assertion is `assertEquals`, which takes two values and checks they are equal and is overloaded to support primitive values. So here we can assert that the size of the `documents` list is 0, as shown in Example 4-23. This produces a slightly better diagnostic as shown in Figure 4-2, you know that the expected value was 0 and the actual value was 1, but it still doesn't give you any meaningful context.

Example 4-23. assertEquals example

```
assertEquals(0, documents.size());
```

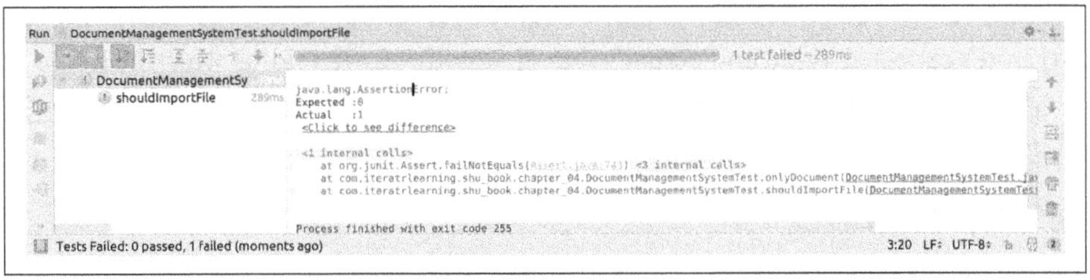

Figure 4-2. Screenshot of assertEquals example failing

The best way of making an assert about the size itself is to use a *matcher* for asserting the collection size as this provides the most descriptive diagnostics. Example 4-24 has our example written in that style and demonstrates the output as well. As Figure 4-3 shows, this is much clearer as to what went wrong without you needing to write any more code.

Example 4-24. assertThat example

```
assertThat(documents, hasSize(0));
```

Figure 4-3. Screenshot of assertThat example failing

What is going on here is that JUnit's `assertThat()` is being used. The method `assert` `That()` takes a value as its first parameter and a `Matcher` as its second. The `Matcher` encapsulates the concept of whether a value matches some property and also its associated diagnostics. The `hasSize` matcher is statically imported from a `Matchers` utility class that contains a bundle of different matchers and checks that the size of a collection is equal to its parameter. These matchers come from the Hamcrest library (*http://hamcrest.org/*), which is a very commonly used Java library that enables cleaner testing.

Another example of how you can build better diagnostics was shown in Example 4-20. Here an `assertEquals` would have given us the diagnostic for the attribute's expected value and actual value. It wouldn't have told us what the name of the attribute was, so this was added into the message string to help us understand failure.

Testing Error Cases

One of the absolute worst and most common mistakes to make when writing software is only to test the beautiful, golden, happy path of your application—the code path that is executed when the sun is shining on you and nothing goes wrong. In practice lots of things can go wrong! If you don't test how your application behaves in these situations, you're not going to end up with software that will work reliably in a production setting.

When it comes to importing documents into our Document Management System there are a couple of error cases that might happen. We might try to import a file that doesn't exist or can't be read, or we might try to import a file that we don't know how to extract text from or read.

Our `DocumentManagementSystemTest` has a couple of tests, shown in Example 4-25, that test these two scenarios. In both cases we try to import a path file that will expose the problem. In order to make an assert about the desired behavior we use the `expected = ` attribute of JUnit's `@Test` annotation. This enables you to say *Hey listen, JUnit, I'm expecting this test to throw an exception, it's of a certain type.*

Example 4-25. Testing for error cases

```
@Test(expected = FileNotFoundException.class)
public void shouldNotImportMissingFile() throws Exception
{
    system.importFile("gobbledygook.txt");
}

@Test(expected = UnknownFileTypeException.class)
public void shouldNotImportUnknownFile() throws Exception
{
    system.importFile(RESOURCES + "unknown.txt");
}
```

You may want an alternative behavior to simply throwing an exception in the case of an error, but it's definitely helpful to know how to assert that an exception is thrown.

Constants

Constants are values that do not change. Let's face it—they are one of the few well-named concepts when it comes to computer programming. The Java programming language doesn't use an explicit `const` keyword like C++ does, but conventionally developers create `static field` fields in order to represent constants. Since many tests consist of examples of how a part of your computer program should be used, they often consist of many constants.

It's a good idea when it comes to constants that have some kind of nonobvious meaning to give them a proper name that can be used within tests. We do that extensively through the `DocumentManagementSystemTest`, and in fact, have a block at the top dedicated to declaring constants, shown in Example 4-26.

Example 4-26. Constants

```
public class DocumentManagementSystemTest
{
    private static final String RESOURCES =
        "src" + File.separator + "test" + File.separator + "resources" + File.separa
tor;
    private static final String LETTER = RESOURCES + "patient.letter";
    private static final String REPORT = RESOURCES + "patient.report";
    private static final String XRAY = RESOURCES + "xray.jpg";
    private static final String INVOICE = RESOURCES + "patient.invoice";
    private static final String JOE_BLOGGS = "Joe Bloggs";
```

Takeaways

- You learned how to build a Document Management System.
- You recognized the different trade-offs between different implementation approaches.
- You understood several principles that drive the design of software.
- You were introduced to the Liskov Substitution Principle as a way to think about inheritance.
- You learned about situations where inheritance wasn't appropriate.

Iterating on You

If you want to extend and solidify the knowledge from this section you could try one of these activities:

- Take the existing sample code and add an implementation for importing prescription documents. A prescription should have a patient, a drug, a quantity, a date, and state the conditions for taking a drug. You should also write a test that checks that the prescription import works.
- Try implementing the Game of Life Kata (*https://oreil.ly/RrxJU*).

Completing the Challenge

Dr. Avaj is really pleased with your Document Management System and she now uses it extensively. Her needs are effectively met by the features because you drove your design from her requirements toward application behavior and into your implementation details. This is a theme that you will return to when TDD is introduced in the next chapter.

CHAPTER 5

The Business Rules Engine

The Challenge

Your business is now doing really well. In fact, you've now scaled to an organization with thousands of employees. This mean you've hired many people for different business functions: marketing, sales, operations, admin, accounting, and so on. You realize that all the business functions have requirements for creating rules that trigger actions depending on some conditions; for example, "notify sales team if prospect's job title is 'CEO.'" You could be asking your tech team to implement each new requirement with bespoke software, but your developers are quite busy working on other products. In order to encourage collaboration between the business team and the tech team, you've decided that you will develop a Business Rules Engine that will enable developers and the business team to write code together. This will allow you to increase productivity and reduce the time it takes to implement new rules because your business team will be able to contribute directly.

The Goal

In this chapter you'll first learn about how to approach a new design problem using test-driven development. You will get an overview about a technique called mocking, which will help specify unit tests. You will then learn about a couple of modern features in Java: local variable type inference and switch expressions. Finally, you'll learn how to develop a friendly API using the Builder pattern and the Interface Segregation Principle.

If at any point you want to look at the source code for this chapter, you can look at the package `com.iteratrlearning.shu_book.chapter_05` in the book's code repository.

Business Rules Engine Requirements

Before you start, let's think about what is it you want to achieve. You'd like to enable nonprogrammers to add or change business logic in their own workflow. For example, a marketing executive may wish to apply a special discount when a prospect is making an inquiry about one of your products and fits certain criteria. An accounting executive may wish to create an alert if expenses are unusually high. These are examples of what you can achieve with a Business Rules Engine. It's essentially software that executes one or more business rules that are often declared using a simple bespoke language. A Business Rules Engine can support multiple different components:

Facts
   The available information to which rules have access

Actions
   The operation you want to perform

Conditions
   These specify when an action should be triggered

Rules
   These specify the business logic you want to execute, essentially grouping facts, conditions, and actions together

The main productivity benefit of a Business Rules Engine is that it enables rules to be maintained, executed, and tested within one place without having to integrate with a main application.

There are many production-ready Java Business Rules Engine such as Drools (*https://www.drools.org*). Typically such an engine conforms to standards such as the *Decision Model and Notation* (DMN) and comes with a centralized rule repository, an editor using a *Graphical User Interface* (GUI), and visualization tools to help maintenance of complex rules. In this chapter, you will develop a minimal viable product for a Business Rules Engine and iterate over it to improve both its functionality and accessibility.

Test Driven Development

Where do you start? The requirements are not set in stone and are expected to evolve so you begin by simply listing the basic features you will need your users to undertake:

- Add an action
- Run the action
- Basic reporting

This translates in the basic API shown in Example 5-1. Each method throws an Unsup portedOperationException indicating it is yet to be implemented.

Example 5-1. Basic API for Business Rules Engine

```java
public class BusinessRuleEngine {

    public void addAction(final Action action) {
        throw new UnsupportedOperationException();
    }

    public int count() {
        throw new UnsupportedOperationException();
    }

    public void run() {
        throw new UnsupportedOperationException();
    }

}
```

An action is simply a piece of code that will be executed. We could use the Runnable interface, but introducing a separate interface Action is more representative of the domain at hand. The Action interface will allow the Business Rules Engine to be decoupled from concrete actions. Since the Action interface only declares a single abstract method, we can annotate it as a functional interface, as shown in Example 5-2.

Example 5-2. The Action interface

```java
@FunctionalInterface
public interface Action {
    void execute();
}
```

Where do we go from here? It's now time to actually write some code—where is the implementation? You will use an approach called *test-driven development* (TDD). The TDD philosophy is to start writing some tests that are going to let you guide the implementation of the code. In other words, you write tests first before the actual implementation. It's a bit like doing the opposite of what you've been doing so far: you wrote the full code for a requirement and then tested it. You will now focus more on the tests.

Why Use TDD?

Why should you take this approach? There are several benefits:

- Writing a test at a time will help you focus and refine the requirements by correctly implementing one thing at a time.
- It's a way to ensure a relevant organization for your code. For example, by writing a test first, you need to think hard about the public interfaces for your code.
- You are building a comprehensive test suite as you iterate through the requirements, which increases confidence that you are matching the requirements and also reduces the scope of bugs.
- You don't write code that you don't need (over-engineer) because you're just writing code that passes the tests.

The TDD Cycle

The TDD approach roughly consists of the following steps in a cycle, as depicted in Figure 5-1:

1. Write a test that fails
2. Run all tests
3. Make the implementation work
4. Run all tests

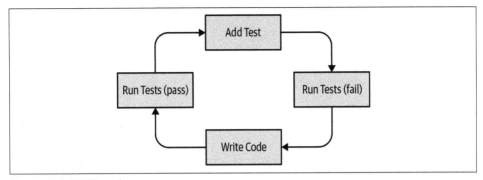

Figure 5-1. TDD cycle

In practice, as part of this process, you must continuously *refactor* your code or it will end up unmaintainable. At this moment you know you have a suite of tests that you can rely on when you introduce changes. Figure 5-2 illustrates this improved TDD process.

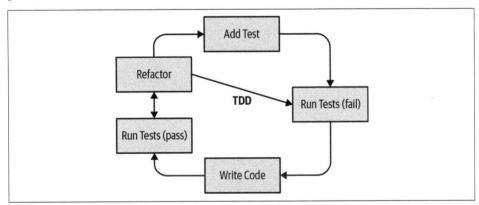

Figure 5-2. TDD with refactoring

In the spirit of TDD, let's start by writing our first tests to verify that `addActions` and count behave correctly, as shown in Example 5-3.

Example 5-3. Basic tests for the Business Rules Engine

```java
@Test
void shouldHaveNoRulesInitially() {
    final BusinessRuleEngine businessRuleEngine = new BusinessRuleEngine();

    assertEquals(0, businessRuleEngine.count());
}

@Test
void shouldAddTwoActions() {
```

```
final BusinessRuleEngine businessRuleEngine = new BusinessRuleEngine();

businessRuleEngine.addAction(() -> {});
businessRuleEngine.addAction(() -> {});

assertEquals(2, businessRuleEngine.count());
}
```

When running the tests, you will see that they fail with an `UnsupportedOperationEx`
`ception`, as shown in Figure 5-3.

Figure 5-3. Failing tests

All tests are failing, but that's fine. It gives us a reproducible test suite that will guide
the implementation of the code. Now can add some implementation code, as shown
in Example 5-4.

Example 5-4. Basic implementation for the Business Rules Engine

```
public class BusinessRuleEngine {

    private final List<Action> actions;

    public BusinessRuleEngine() {
        this.actions = new ArrayList<>();
    }

    public void addAction(final Action action) {
        this.actions.add(action);
    }

    public int count() {
        return this.actions.size();
    }

    public void run(){
        throw new UnsupportedOperationException();
    }
}
```

You can now rerun the tests and they are passing! However, there's one crucial operation missing. How do we write a test for the method run? Unfortunately, `run()` does

not return any result. We are going to need a new technique called *mocking* to verify that the method run() operates correctly.

Mocking

Mocking is a technique that will allow you to verify that when the method run() is executed, each action that was added to the Business Rules Engine is actually executed. At the moment it is difficult to do because both the methods run() in Busi nessRuleEngine and perform() in Action are returning void. We have no way to write an assertion! Mocking is covered in detail in Chapter 6, but you will get a brief overview now so you are able to progress with writing a test. You'll be using Mockito, which is a popular mocking library for Java. At its simplest you can do two things:

1. Create a mock.
2. Verify that a method is called.

So how do you get started? You will need to import the library first:

```
import static org.mockito.Mockito.*;
```

This import allows you to use the methods mock() and verify(). The static method mock() allows you to create a mock object which you can then verify that certain behaviors happen. The method verify() allows you to set up assertions that a particular method is invoked. Example 5-5 shows an example.

Example 5-5. Mocking and verifying interaction with an Action object

```
@Test
void shouldExecuteOneAction() {
        final BusinessRuleEngine businessRuleEngine = new BusinessRuleEngine();
        final Action mockAction = mock(Action.class);

        businessRuleEngine.addAction(mockAction);
        businessRuleEngine.run();

        verify(mockAction).perform();
}
```

The unit test creates a mock object for Action. This is done by passing the class as argument to the mock method. Next, you have the *when* part of your test where you invoke behaviors. Here we are adding the action and executing the method run(). Finally, you have the *then* part of the unit tests, which sets up assertions. In this case, we verify that the method perform() on the Action object was invoked.

If you run this test it will fail as expected with a UnsupportedOperationException. What if the body of run() is empty? You will receive a new exception trace:

```
Wanted but not invoked:
action.perform();
-> at BusinessRuleEngineTest.shouldExecuteOneAction(BusinessRuleEngineTest.java:
35)
Actually, there were zero interactions with this mock.
```

This error is coming from Mockito and tells you that the method perform() was never invoked. It's now time to write the correct implementation for the method run(), as shown in Example 5-6.

Example 5-6. The run() method implementation

```
public void run() {
    this.actions.forEach(Action::perform);
}
```

Re-run the tests and you will now see the test passing. Mockito was able to verify that when the Business Rules Engine is running, the method perform() on the Action object should be invoked. Mockito allows you to specify sophisticated verification logic such as how many times a method should be invoked, with certain arguments, etc. You will learn more about this in Chapter 6.

Adding Conditions

You have to admit that so far the Business Rules Engine is pretty limiting. You can only declare simple actions. However, in practice, the users of the Business Rules Engine will need to execute actions based on certain conditions. These conditions will be dependent on some facts. For example, notify the sales team *only if the prospect's job title is CEO*.

Modeling State

You may start by writing code that adds an action and refers to a local variable using an anonymous class as shown in Example 5-7, or using a lambda expression as shown in Example 5-8.

Example 5-7. Adding an action using an anonymous class

```
// this object could be created from a form
final Customer customer = new Customer("Mark", "CEO");

businessRuleEngine.addAction(new Action() {

    @Override
    public void perform() {
        if ("CEO".equals(customer.getJobTitle())) {
            Mailer.sendEmail("sales@company.com", "Relevant customer: " + customer);
```

```
        }
    }
});
```

Example 5-8. Adding an action using a lambda expression

```
// this object could be created from a form
final Customer customer = new Customer("Mark", "CEO");

businessRuleEngine.addAction(() -> {
    if ("CEO".equals(customer.getJobTitle())) {
        Mailer.sendEmail("sales@company.com", "Relevant customer: " + customer);
    }
});
```

However, this approach is inconvenient for several reasons:

1. How do you test the action? It's not an independent piece of functionality; it has a hardcoded dependency on the customer object.

2. The customer object is not grouped with the action. It is a sort of external state that is shared around, leading to a confusing mix of responsibilities.

So what do we need? We need to encapsulate the state that is available to actions within the Business Rules Engine. Let's model these requirements by introducing a new class called `Facts`, which will represent the state available as part of the Business Rules Engine, and an updated `Action` interface that can operate on facts. An updated unit test is shown in Example 5-9. The unit test checks that when the Business Rules Engine runs, the specified action is actually invoked with the `Facts` object passed as an argument.

Example 5-9. Testing an action with facts

```
@Test
public void shouldPerformAnActionWithFacts() {
    final Action mockAction = mock(Action.class);
    final Facts mockFacts = mock(Facts.class);
    final BusinessRuleEngine businessRuleEngine = new BusinessRuleEngine(mocked
Facts);

    businessRuleEngine.addAction(mockAction);
    businessRuleEngine.run();

    verify(mockAction).perform(mockFacts);
}
```

To follow the TDD philosophy, this test will initially fail. You always need to run the tests to begin with to ensure that they fail, otherwise you may write a test that accidentally passes. To make the test pass you will need to update the API and implementation code. First, you'll introduce the Facts class, which allows you to store a fact represented as a key and a value. The benefit of introducing a separate Facts class for modeling state is that you can control the operations available to your users by providing a public API, and also unit test the behavior of the class. For the time being, the Facts class will only support String keys and String values. The code for the Facts class is shown in Example 5-10. We chose the names getFact and addFact because they better represent the domain at hand (working with facts) rather than getValue and setValue.

Example 5-10. The Facts class

```
public class Facts {

    private final Map<String, String> facts = new HashMap<>();

    public String getFact(final String name) {
        return this.facts.get(name);
    }

    public void addFact(final String name, final String value) {
        this.facts.put(name, value);
    }
}
```

You'll now need to refactor the Action interface so that the perform() method can use a Facts object passed as an argument. This way it's clear the facts are available within the context of the single Action (Example 5-11).

Example 5-11. The Action interface that takes facts

```
@FunctionalInterface
public interface Action {
    void perform(Facts facts);
}
```

Finally, you can now update the BusinessRuleEngine class to utilize the facts and the updated Action's perform() method as shown in Example 5-12.

Example 5-12. BusinessRuleEngine with facts

```
public class BusinessRuleEngine {

    private final List<Action> actions;
```

```
    private final Facts facts;

    public BusinessRuleEngine(final Facts facts) {
        this.facts = facts;
        this.actions = new ArrayList<>();
    }

    public void addAction(final Action action) {
        this.actions.add(action);
    }

    public int count() {
        return this.actions.size();
    }

    public void run() {
        this.actions.forEach(action -> action.perform(facts));
    }
}
```

Now that the Facts object is available to actions, you can specify arbitrary logic in your code that looks up the Facts object as shown in Example 5-13.

Example 5-13. An action utilizing the facts

```
businessRuleEngine.addAction(facts -> {
    final String jobTitle = facts.getFact("jobTitle");
    if ("CEO".equals(jobTitle)) {
        final String name = facts.getFact("name");
        Mailer.sendEmail("sales@company.com", "Relevant customer: " + name);
    }
});
```

Let's look at some more examples. This is also a good opportunity to introduce two recent features in Java, which we explore in order:

- Local variable type inference
- Switch expressions

Local Variable Type Inference

Java 10 introduced variable local type inference. Type inference is the idea that the compiler can figure out the static types for you so you don't have to type them. You saw an example of type inference earlier in Example 5-10 when you wrote

```
    Map<String, String> facts = new HashMap<>();
```

instead of

```
Map<String, String> facts = new HashMap<String, String>();
```

This is a feature that was introduced in Java 7 called the *diamond operator*. Essentially, you can omit the type parameters of generics (in this case String, String) in an expression when its context determines them. In the preceding code, the lefthand side of the assignment indicates the keys and values of the Map should be Strings.

Since Java 10, type inference has been extended to work on local variables. For example, the code in Example 5-14 can be rewritten using the var keyword and local variable type inference shown in Example 5-15.

Example 5-14. Local variable declaration with explicit types

```
Facts env = new Facts();
BusinessRuleEngine businessRuleEngine = new BusinessRuleEngine(env);
```

Example 5-15. Local variable type inference

```
var env = new Facts();
var businessRuleEngine = new BusinessRuleEngine(env);
```

By using the var keyword in the code shown in Example 5-15, the variable env still has a static type Facts and the variable businessRuleEngine still has the static type BusinessRuleEngine.

> A variable declared using the var keyword is not made final. For example, this code:
>
> ```
> final Facts env = new Facts();
> ```
>
> is not strictly equivalent to:
>
> ```
> var env = new Facts();
> ```
>
> You can still assign another value to the variable env after declaring it using var. You'd have to explicitly add the final keyword as follows in front of the variable env for it to be final:
>
> ```
> final var env = new Facts()
> ```
>
> In the rest of the chapters, we simply use the var keyword without final for brevity as it is in the spirit of code conciseness. When we explicitly declare the type of a variable, we use the final keyword.

Type inference helps reduce the amount of time taken to write Java code. However, should you use this feature all the time? It's worth remembering that developers spend more time reading code than writing it. In other words, you should think about optimizing for ease of reading over ease of writing. The extent to which var improves this will always be subjective. You should always be focusing on what helps your teammates read your code, so if they are happy reading code with var then you should use it, otherwise not. For example, here we can refactor the code in Example 5-13 to use local variable type inference to tidy up the code as shown in Example 5-16.

Example 5-16. An action utilizing the facts and local variable type inference

```
businessRuleEngine.addAction(facts -> {
    var jobTitle = facts.getFact("jobTitle");
    if ("CEO".equals(jobTitle)) {
        var name = facts.getFact("name");
        Mailer.sendEmail("sales@company.com", "Relevant customer: " + name);
    }
});
```

Switch Expressions

So far you've only set up actions with exactly one condition to handle. This is pretty limiting. For example, say you work with your sales team. They may record on their *Customer Relationship Management* (CRM) system different deals with different amounts that have different stages. A deal stage may be represented as an enum Stage with values including LEAD, INTERESTED, EVALUATING, CLOSED, as shown in Example 5-17.

Example 5-17. Enum representing different deal stages

```
public enum Stage {
    LEAD, INTERESTED, EVALUATING, CLOSED
}
```

Depending on the stage of the deal you can assign a rule that gives you the probability of winning the deal. Consequently, you can help the sales team with generating a forecast. Say for a particular team, LEAD has 20% probability to convert, then a deal at stage LEAD with amount of 1000USD will have a forecasted amount of 200USD. Let's create an action to model these rules and return a forecasted amount for a particular deal as shown in Example 5-18.

Example 5-18. A rule to calculate a forecast amount for a specific deal

```
businessRuleEngine.addAction(facts -> {
    var forecastedAmount = 0.0;
    var dealStage = Stage.valueOf(facts.getFact("stage"));
    var amount = Double.parseDouble(facts.getFact("amount"));
    if(dealStage == Stage.LEAD){
        forecastedAmount = amount * 0.2;
    } else if (dealStage == Stage.EVALUATING) {
```

```
        forecastedAmount = amount * 0.5;
    } else if(dealStage == Stage.INTERESTED) {
        forecastedAmount = amount * 0.8;
    } else if(dealStage == Stage.CLOSED) {
        forecastedAmount = amount;
    }
    facts.addFact("forecastedAmount", String.valueOf(forecastedAmount));
});
```

The code shown in Example 5-18 is essentially providing a value for each enum value available. A preferred language construct is the switch statement as it's more succinct. This is shown in Example 5-19.

Example 5-19. A rule to calculate a forecast amount for a specific deal using a switch statement

```
switch (dealStage) {
    case LEAD:
        forecastedAmount = amount * 0.2;
        break;
    case EVALUATING:
        forecastedAmount = amount * 0.5;
        break;
    case INTERESTED:
        forecastedAmount = amount * 0.8;
        break;
    case CLOSED:
        forecastedAmount = amount;
        break;
}
```

Note all the break statements in the code in Example 5-19. The break statement ensures that the next block in the switch statement is not executed. If you forget the break by accident, then the code still compiles and you get what's called a *fall-through* behavior. In other words, the next block is executed and this can lead to subtle bugs. Since Java 12 (using the language feature preview mode) you can rewrite this to avoid the fall-through behavior and multiple breaks by using a different syntax for switch. switch can now be used as an expression, as illustrated in Example 5-20.

Example 5-20. Switch expression with no fall-through behavior

```
var forecastedAmount = amount * switch (dealStage) {
    case LEAD -> 0.2;
    case EVALUATING -> 0.5;
    case INTERESTED -> 0.8;
    case CLOSED -> 1;
}
```

Another benefit of this enhanced switch form, besides increased readability, is *exhaustiveness*. This means that when you use switch with an enum, the Java compiler checks that for all enum values there's a corresponding switch label. For example, if you forget to handle the CLOSED case, the Java compiler would produce the following error:

```
error: the switch expression does not cover all possible input values.
```

You can rewrite the overall action using a switch expression as shown in Example 5-21.

Example 5-21. A rule to calculate a forecast amount for a specific deal

```
businessRuleEngine.addAction(facts -> {
    var dealStage = Stage.valueOf(facts.getFact("stage"));
    var amount = Double.parseDouble(facts.getFact("amount"));
    var forecastedAmount = amount * switch (dealStage) {
        case LEAD -> 0.2;
        case EVALUATING -> 0.5;
        case INTERESTED -> 0.8;
        case CLOSED -> 1;
    }
    facts.addFact("forecastedAmount", String.valueOf(forecastedAmount));
});
```

Interface Segregation Principle

We would now like to develop an *inspector tool* that allows users of the Business Rules Engine to inspect the status of possible actions and conditions. For example, we would like to evaluate each action and associated condition in order to log them without actually performing the action. How do we go about this? The current Action interface is not sufficient because it doesn't separate the code performed versus the condition that triggers that code. At the moment there's no way to separate out the condition from the action code. To make up for this, we could introduce an enhanced Action interface that has a built-in functionality for evaluating the condition. For example, we could create an interface ConditionalAction that includes a new method evaluate() as shown in Example 5-22.

Example 5-22. ConditionalAction interface

```
public interface ConditionalAction {
    boolean evaluate(Facts facts);
    void perform(Facts facts);
}
```

We can now implement a basic Inspector class that takes a list of ConditionalAction objects and evaluates them based on some facts, as shown in Example 5-23. The

Inspector returns a list of reports that captures the facts, the conditional action, and the result. The implementation for the Report class is shown in Example 5-24.

Example 5-23. An Inspector of conditions

```java
public class Inspector {

    private final List<ConditionalAction> conditionalActionList;

    public Inspector(final ConditionalAction...conditionalActions) {
        this.conditionalActionList = Arrays.asList(conditionalActions);
    }

    public List<Report> inspect(final Facts facts) {
        final List<Report> reportList = new ArrayList<>();
        for (ConditionalAction conditionalAction : conditionalActionList) {
            final boolean conditionResult = conditionalAction.evaluate(facts);
            reportList.add(new Report(facts, conditionalAction, conditionResult));
        }
        return reportList;
    }
}
```

Example 5-24. The Report class

```java
public class Report {

    private final ConditionalAction conditionalAction;
    private final Facts facts;
    private final boolean isPositive;

    public Report(final Facts facts,
                  final ConditionalAction conditionalAction,
                  final boolean isPositive) {
        this.facts = facts;
        this.conditionalAction = conditionalAction;
        this.isPositive = isPositive;
    }

    public ConditionalAction getConditionalAction() {
        return conditionalAction;
    }

    public Facts getFacts() {
        return facts;
    }

    public boolean isPositive() {
        return isPositive;
    }
```

```
    @Override
    public String toString() {
        return "Report{" +
                "conditionalAction=" + conditionalAction +
                ", facts=" + facts +
                ", result=" + isPositive +
                '}';
    }
}
```

How would we go about testing the `Inspector`? You may start by writing a simple unit test as shown in Example 5-25. This test highlights a fundamental issue with our current design. In fact, the `ConditionalAction` interface breaks the *Interface Segregation Principle* (ISP).

Example 5-25. Highlighting ISP violation

```
public class InspectorTest {

    @Test
    public void inspectOneConditionEvaluatesTrue() {

        final Facts facts = new Facts();
        facts.setFact("jobTitle", "CEO");
        final ConditionalAction conditionalAction = new JobTitleCondition();
        final Inspector inspector = new Inspector(conditionalAction);

        final List<Report> reportList = inspector.inspect(facts);

        assertEquals(1, reportList.size());
        assertEquals(true, reportList.get(0).isPositive());
    }

    private static class JobTitleCondition implements ConditionalAction {

        @Override
        public void perform(Facts facts) {
            throw new UnsupportedOperationException();
        }

        @Override
        public boolean evaluate(Facts facts) {
            return "CEO".equals(facts.getFact("jobTitle"));
        }
    }
}
```

What is the Interface Segregation Principle? You may notice that the implementation of the `perform` method is empty. In fact, it throws an `UnsupportedOperationExcep` tion. This is a situation where you are coupled to an interface (`ConditionalAction`) that provides more than what you need. In this case, we just want a way to model a condition—something that evaluates to either true or false. Nonetheless, we are forced to depend on the `perform()` method because it is part of the interface.

This general idea is the foundation of the Interface Segregation Principle. It makes the case that no class should be forced to depend on methods it does not use because this introduces unnecessary coupling. In Chapter 2, you learned about another principle, the *Single Responsibility Principle* (SRP), which promotes high cohesion. The SRP is a general design guideline that a class has responsibility over a single functionality and there should be only one reason for it to change. Although the ISP may sound like the same idea, it takes a different view. The ISP focuses on the user of an interface rather than its design. In other words, if an interface ends up very large, it may be that the user of that interface sees some behaviors it doesn't care for, which causes unnecessary coupling.

To provide a solution that meets the Interface Segregation Principle, we are encouraged to separate out concepts in smaller interface that can evolve separately. This idea essentially promotes higher cohesion. Separating out interfaces also provides an opportunity for introducing names that are closer to the domain at hand, such as `Condition` and `Action`, which we explore in the next section.

Designing a Fluent API

So far we've provided a way for our users to add actions with complex conditions. These conditions were created using the enhanced switch statement. However, for business users the syntax isn't as friendly as it could be to specify simple conditions. We'd like to allow them to add rules (a condition and an action) in a way that matches their domain and is simpler to specify. In this section, you will learn about the Builder pattern and how to develop your own Fluent API to address this problem.

What Is a Fluent API?

A Fluent API is an API that is explicitly tailored for a specific domain so that you can solve a specific problem more intuitively. It also embraces the idea of chaining method calls to specify a more complex operation. There are several high-profile Fluent APIs you may be already familiar with:

- The Java Streams API (*https://oreil.ly/549wN*) allows you to specify data processing queries in a way that reads more like the problem you need to solve.

- Spring Integration (*https://oreil.ly/rMIMD*) offers a Java API to specify enterprise integration patterns using a vocabulary close to the domain of enterprise integration patterns.

- jOOQ (*https://www.jooq.org/*) offers a library to interact with different databases using an intuitive API.

Modeling the Domain

So what is it that we want to simply for our business users? We'd like to help them specify a simple combination of "when some condition holds," "then do something" as a rule. There are three concepts in this domain:

Condition
    A condition applied on certain facts that will evaluate to either true or false.

Action
    A specific set of operations or code to execute.

Rule
    This is a condition and an action together. The action only runs if the condition is true.

Now that we've defined the concepts in the domain, we translate it into Java! Let's first define the `Condition` interface and reuse our existing `Action` interface as shown in Example 5-26. Note that we could have also used the `java.util.function.Predi cate` interface available since Java 8, but the name `Condition` better represents our domain.

 Names are very important in programming because good names help you understand the problem that your code is solving. Names are in many cases more important than the "shape" of the interface (in terms of its parameters and return types), because the names convey contextual information to humans reading the code.

Example 5-26. The Condition interface

```
@FunctionalInterface
public interface Condition {
    boolean evaluate(Facts facts);
}
```

Now the remaining question is how to model the concept of a rule? We can define a interface `Rule` with an operation `perform()`. This will allow you to provide different implementations of a `Rule`. A suitable default implementation of this interface is a class `DefaultRule`, which will hold a `Condition` and `Action` object together with the appropriate logic to perform a rule as shown in Example 5-27.

Example 5-27. Modeling the concept of a rule

```
@FunctionalInterface
interface Rule {
    void perform(Facts facts);
}

public class DefaultRule implements Rule {

    private final Condition condition;
    private final Action action;

    public Rule(final Condition condition, final Action action) {
        this.condition = condition;
        this.action = action;
    }

    public void perform(final Facts facts) {
        if(condition.evaluate(facts)){
            action.execute(facts);
        }
    }
}
```

How do we create new rules using all these different elements? You can see an example in Example 5-28.

Example 5-28. Building a rule

```
final Condition condition = (Facts facts) -> "CEO".equals(facts.getFact("jobTi
tle"));
final Action action = (Facts facts) -> {
    var name = facts.getFact("name");
    Mailer.sendEmail("sales@company.com", "Relevant customer!!!: " + name);
};

final Rule rule = new DefaultRule(condition, action);
```

Builder Pattern

However, even though the code uses names that are close to our domain (Condition, Action, Rule), this code is fairly manual. The user has to instantiate separate objects and assemble things together. Let's introduce what's called the *Builder pattern* to improve the process of creating a Rule object with the appropriate condition and action. The purpose of this pattern is to allow the creation of an object in a simpler manner. The Builder pattern essentially deconstructs the parameters of a constructor and instead provides methods to supply each of the parameters. The benefit of this approach is that it allows you to declare methods with names that are suitable to the domain at hand. For example, in our case we'd like to use the vocabulary when and then. The code in Example 5-29 shows how to set up the Builder pattern to build a DefaultRule object. We've introduced a method when(), which supplies the condition. The method when() returns this (i.e., the current instance), which will allow us to chain up further methods. We've also introduced a method then(), which will supply the action. The method then() also returns this, which allows us to further chain a method. Finally, the method createRule() is responsible for the creation of the DefaultRule object.

Example 5-29. Builder pattern for a Rule

```java
public class RuleBuilder {
    private Condition condition;
    private Action action;

    public RuleBuilder when(final Condition condition) {
        this.condition = condition;
        return this;
    }

    public RuleBuilder then(final Action action) {
        this.action = action;
        return this;
    }

    public Rule createRule() {
        return new DefaultRule(condition, action);
    }
}
```

Using this new class, you can create RuleBuilder and configure a Rule using the methods when(), then(), and createRule() as shown in Example 5-30. This idea of chaining methods is a key aspect of designing a Fluent API.

Example 5-30. Using the RuleBuilder

```java
Rule rule = new RuleBuilder()
        .when(facts -> "CEO".equals(facts.getFact("jobTitle")))
        .then(facts -> {
            var name = facts.getFact("name");
            Mailer.sendEmail("sales@company.com", "Relevant customer: " + name);
        })
        .createRule();
```

This code looks more like a query and it leverages the domain at hand: the notion of a rule, when(), and then() as built-in constructs. But it's not entirely satisfactory because there are still two awkward constructs the user of your API will have to encounter:

- Instantiate an "empty" `RuleBuilder`
- Call the method `createRule()`

We can improve this by coming up with a slightly improved API. There are three possible improvements:

- We'll make the constructor private so that it can not be invoked explicitly by a user. This means that we will need to come up with a different entry point for our API.
- We can make the method `when()` static so it's invoked directly and essentially short circuits the invocation to the old constructor. In addition, a static factor method improves discoverability of what's the right method to use to set up `Rule` objects.
- The method `then()` will become responsible for the final creation of our `DefaultRule` object.

Example 5-31 shows the improved `RuleBuilder`.

Example 5-31. Improved RuleBuilder

```
public class RuleBuilder {
    private final Condition condition;

    private RuleBuilder(final Condition condition) {
        this.condition = condition;
    }

    public static RuleBuilder when(final Condition condition) {
        return new RuleBuilder(condition);
    }

    public Rule then(final Action action) {
        return new DefaultRule(condition, action);
    }
}
```

You can now simply create rules by starting with the `RuleBuilder.when()` method followed by the `then()` method as shown in Example 5-32.

Example 5-32. Using the improved RuleBuilder

```
final Rule ruleSendEmailToSalesWhenCEO = RuleBuilder
        .when(facts -> "CEO".equals(facts.getFact("jobTitle")))
        .then(facts -> {
            var name = facts.getFact("name");
```

```
        Mailer.sendEmail("sales@company.com", "Relevant customer!!!: " + name);
    });
```

Now that we've refactored the `RuleBuilder`, we can refactor the Business Rules Engine to support rules instead of just actions, as shown in Example 5-33.

Example 5-33. Updated Business Rules Engine

```
public class BusinessRuleEngine {

    private final List<Rule> rules;
    private final Facts facts;

    public BusinessRuleEngine(final Facts facts) {
        this.facts = facts;
        this.rules = new ArrayList<>();
    }

    public void addRule(final Rule rule) {
        this.rules.add(rule);
    }

    public void run() {
        this.rules.forEach(rule -> rule.perform(facts));
    }

}
```

Takeaways

- The test-driven development philosophy starts with writing some tests that are going to let you guide the implementation of the code.
- Mocking allows you to write unit tests that assert that certain behaviors are triggered.
- Java supports local variable type inferences and switch expressions.
- The Builder pattern helps design a user-friendly API for instantiating complex objects.
- The Interface Segregation Principle helps promote high cohesion by reducing dependence on unnecessary methods. This is achieved by breaking up large interfaces into smaller cohesive interfaces so that users only see what they need.

Iterating on You

If you want to extend and solidify the knowledge from this chapter you could try one of these activities:

- Enhance the `Rule` and `RuleBuilder` to support a name and description.
- Enhance the `Facts` class so the facts can be loaded from a JSON file.
- Enhance the Business Rules Engine to support rules having multiple conditions.
- Enhance the Business Rules Engine to support rules with different priorities.

Completing the Challenge

Your business is booming and your company has adopted the Business Rules Engine as part of its workflow! You are now looking for your next idea and want to put your software development skills to something new that will help the world rather than just your company. It's time to jump to the next chapter—Twootr!

CHAPTER 6

Twootr

The Challenge

Joe was an excited young chap, keen to tell me all about his new startup idea. He was on a mission to help people communicate better and faster. He enjoyed blogging but wondered about how to get people to blog more frequently in smaller amounts. He was calling it micro-blogging. The big idea was that if you restricted the size of the messages to 140 characters that people would post little and often rather than in big messages.

We asked Joe if he felt that this restriction would encourage people to just post short, pithy statements that didn't really mean anything. He said "Yolo!" We asked Joe how he was going to make money. He said "Yolo!" We asked Joe what he planned to call the product. He said "Twootr!" We thought it sounded like a cool and original idea, so we decided to help him build his product.

The Goal

In this chapter you will learn about the big picture of putting a software application together. A lot of the previous apps in this book were smaller examples—batch jobs that would run on the command line. Twootr is a server-side Java application, similar to the kind of application that most Java developers write.

In this chapter you'll have the opportunity to learn about a number of different skills:

- How to take a big picture description and break it down into different architectural concerns
- How to use test doubles to isolate and test interactions from different components within your codebase

- How to think outside-in—to go from requirements through to the core of your application domain

At several places in this chapter we will also talk not only about the final design of the software, but how we got there. There are a few places where we show how certain methods iteratively evolved over the development of the project in response to an expanding list of implemented features. This will give you a feel for how software projects can evolve in reality, rather than simply presenting an idealized final design abstract of its thought process.

Twootr Requirements

The previous applications that you've seen in this book are all line-of-business applications that process data and documents. Twootr, on the other hand, is a user-facing application. When we talked to Joe about the requirements for his system, it became apparent that he had refined his ideas a bit. Each micro-blog from a user would be called a *twoot* and users would have a constant stream of twoots. In order to see what other users were twooting about, you would *follow* those users.

Joe had brainstormed some different use cases—scenarios in which his users use the service. This is the functionality that we need to get working in order to help Joe achieve his goal of helping people communicate better:

- Users log in to Twootr with a unique user ID and password.
- Each user has a set of other users that they follow.
- Users can send a twoot, and any followers who are logged in should immediately see the twoot.
- When users log in they should see all the twoots from their followers since they last logged in.
- Users should be able to delete twoots. Deleted twoots should no longer be visible to followers.
- Users should be able to log in from a mobile phone or a website.

The first step in explaining how we go about implementing a solution fit for Joe's needs is to overview and outline the big-picture design choices that we face.

Design Overview

If at any point you want to look at the source code for this chapter, you can look at the package com.iteratrlearning.shu_book.chapter_06 in the book's code repository.

If you want to see the project in action, you should run the Twootr Server class from your IDE and then browser to *http://localhost: 8000*.

If we pick out the last requirement and consider it first then it strikes us that, in contrast to many of the other systems in this book, we need to build a system that has many computers communicating together in some way. This is because our users may be running the software on different computers—for example, one user may load the Twootr website on their desktop at home and another may run Twootr on a mobile phone. How will these different user interfaces talk to each other?

The most common approach taken by software developers trying to approach this kind of problem is to use the *client-server* model. In this approach to developing distributed applications we group our computers into two main groups. We have *clients* who request the use of some kind of service and *servers* who provide the service in question. So in our case our clients would be something like a website or a mobile phone application that provides a UI through which we can communicate with the Twootr server. The server would process the majority of the business logic and send and receive twoots to different clients. This is shown in Figure 6-1.

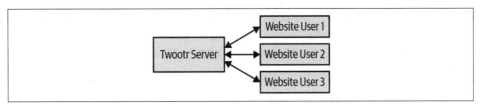

Figure 6-1. Client-server model

It was clear from the requirements and talking to Joe that a key part of this system working was the ability to immediately view twoots from users you follow. This means that the user interface would have to have the ability to receive twoots from the server as well as send them. There are, in big-picture terms, two different styles of communication that can be used to achieve this goal: pull-based or push-based.

Pull-Based

In a *pull-based communication* style the client makes a request to the server and queries it for information. This style of communication is often called a point-to-point style or a request-response style of communication. This is a particularly common communication style, used by most of the web. When you load a website it will make an HTTP request to some server, pulling the page's data. Pull-based communication styles are useful when the client controls what content to load. For example, if you're browsing wikipedia you control which pages you're interested in reading about or seeing next and the content responses are sent back to you. This is shown in Figure 6-2.

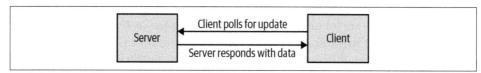

Figure 6-2. Pull communications

Push-Based

Another approach is a *push-based communication* style. This could be referred to as a reactive or event-driven communication approach. In this model, streams of events are emitted by a publisher and many subscribers listen to them. So instead of each communication being 1 to 1, they are 1 to many. This is a really useful model for systems where different components need to talk in terms of ongoing communication patterns of multiple events. For example, if you're designing a stock market exchange then different companies want to see updated prices, or ticks, constantly rather than having to make a new request every time they want to see a new tick. This is shown in Figure 6-3.

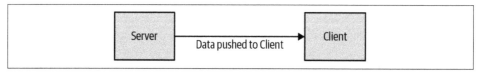

Figure 6-3. Push communications

In the case of Twootr, an event-driven communication style seems most suitable for the application as it mainly consists of ongoing streams of twoots. The events in this model would be the twoots themselves. We could definitely still design the application in terms of a request-response communication style. If we went down this route, however, the client would have to be regularly polling the server and asking with a request saying, "Hey, has anyone twooted since my last request?" In an event-driven style you simply subscribe to your events—i.e., follow another user—and the server pushes the twoots that you're interested in to the client.

This choice of an event-driven communication style influences the rest of the application design from here on in. When we write code that implements the main class of our application, we'll be receiving events and sending them. How to receive and send events determines the patterns within our code and also how we write tests for our code.

From Events to Design

Having said that, we're building a client-server application—this chapter will focus on the server-side component rather than the client component. In "User Interface" on page 163 you will see how a client can be developed for this codebase, and an example client is implemented in the code samples that go with this book. There are two reasons why we focus on the server-side component. First, this is a book on how to write software in Java, which is extensively used on the server side but not so widely on the client side. Second, the server side is where the business logic lies: the brains of the application. The client side is a very simple codebase that just needs to bind a UI to publishing and subscribing events.

Communication

Having established that we want to send and receive events, a common next step in our design would be to pick some kind of technology to send those messages to or from our client to our server. There are lots of choices in this area, and here are a few routes that we could go down:

- WebSockets are a modern, lightweight communications protocol to provide duplex (two-way) communication of events over a TCP stream. They are often used for event-driven communication between a web browser and a web server and is supported by recent browser releases.

- Hosted cloud-based message queues such as Amazon Simple Queue Service are an increasingly popular choice for broadcasting and receiving events. A message queue is a way of performing inter-process communication by sending messages that can either be received by a single process of a group of processes. The benefit of being a hosted service is that your company doesn't have to expend effort on ensuring that they are reliably hosted.

- There are many good open source message transports or message queues, such as Aeron, ZeroMQ, and AMPQ implementations. Many of these open source projects avoid vendor lock-in, though they may limit your choice of client to something that can interact with a message queue. For example, they wouldn't be appropriate if your client is a web browser.

That's far from an exhaustive list, and as you can see different technologies have different trade-offs and use cases. It might be the case that, for your own program, you pick one of these technologies. At a later date you decide that it's not the right choice and want to pick another. It might be that you wish to choose different types of communications technologies for different types of connecting clients. Either way, making that decision at the beginning of your project and being forced to live with it forever isn't a great architectural decision. Later in this chapter we will see how it's possible to abstract away this architectural choice to avoid a big-mistake-up-front architectural decision.

It's even possibly the case that you may want to combine different communications approaches; for example, by using different communications approaches for different types of client. Figure 6-4 visualizes using WebSockets to communicate with a website and Android push notifications for your Android mobile app.

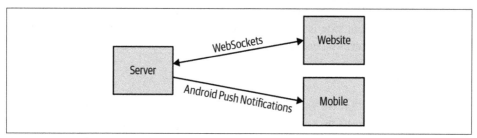

Figure 6-4. Different communications approaches

GUI

Coupling the choice of UI communications technology or your UI to your core server-side business logic also has several other disadvantages:

- It is difficult and slow to test. Every test would have to test the system by publishing and subscribing to events running in parallel with the main server.

- It breaks the Single Responsibility Principle that we talked about in Chapter 2.

- It assumes that we're going to have a UI as our client. At first this might be a solid assumption for Twootr, but in the glorious future we might wish to have interactive artificially intelligent chat bots helping solve user problems. Or twooting cat GIFs at least!

The takeaway from this is that we would be prudent to introduce some kind of abstraction to decouple the messaging for our UI from the core business logic. We need an interface through which we can send messages to the client and an interface through which we can receive messages from the client.

Persistence

There are similar concerns at the other side of the application. How should we store the data for Twootr? We have many choices to pick from:

- Plain-text files that we can index and search ourselves. It's easy to see what has been logged and avoids a dependency on another application.
- A traditional SQL database. It's well tested and understood, with strong querying support.
- A NoSQL database. There are a variety of different databases here with differing use cases, query languages, and data storage models.

We don't really know which to pick at the beginning of our software project and our needs may evolve over time. We really want to decouple our choice of storage back-end from the rest of our application. There's a similarity between these different issues—both are about wanting to avoid coupling yourself to a specific technology.

The Hexagonal Architecture

In fact, there's a name for a more general architectural style here that helps us solve this problem. It's called the *Ports and Adapters* or *Hexagonal* architecture and was originally introduced by Alister Cockburn (*https://oreil.ly/wJO17*). The idea, shown in Figure 6-5, is that the core of your application is the business logic that you're writing, and you want to keep different implementation choices separate from this core logic.

Whenever you have a technology-specific concern that you want to decouple from the core of your business logic, you introduce a *port*. Events from the outside world arrive at and depart from your business logic core through a port. An *adapter* is the technology-specific implementation code that plugs into the port. For example, we may have a port for publishing and subscribing to UI events and a WebSocket adapter that talks to a web browser.

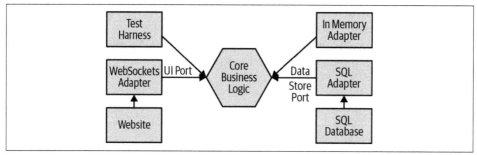

Figure 6-5. Hexagonal architecture

There are other components within a system for which you might want to create a port and adapter abstraction. One thing that might be relevant to an expanded Twootr implementation is a notification system. Informing users that they have a lot of twoots they might be interested in logging in and seeing would be a port. You may wish to implement this with an adapter for email or text messages.

Another example port that comes to mind is authentication services. You may wish to start off with an adapter that just stores the usernames and passwords, later replacing it with an OAuth backend or tying it to some other system. In the Twootr implementation that this chapter describes we don't go so far as to abstract out authentication. This is because our requirements and initial brainstorming session haven't come up with a good reason why we might want different authentication adapters as of yet.

You might be wondering how you separate what should be a port and what should be part of the core domain. At one extreme you could have hundreds or even thousands of ports in your application and nearly everything could be abstracted out of the core domain. At the other extreme you could have none at all. Where you decide your application should live on this sliding scale is a matter of personal judgment and circumstance: there are no rules.

A good principle to help you decide might be to think of anything that is critical to the business problem that you're solving as living inside the core of the application and anything that is technology specific or involves communicating with the outside world as living outside the core application. That is the principle that we've used in this application. So business logic is part of our core domain, but responsibility for persistence and event-driven communication with the UI are hidden behind ports.

Where to Begin

We could proceed with outlining the design in more and more detail at this stage, designing more elaborate diagrams and deciding what functionality should live in what class. We've never found that to be a terribly productive approach to writing software. It tends to result in lots of assumptions and design decisions being pushed down into little boxes in an architecture diagram that turn out to be not so little. Diving straight into coding with no thought to overall design is unlikely to result in the best software, either. Software development needs *just enough upfront design* to avoid it collapsing into chaos, but architecture without coding enough bits to make it real can quickly become sterile and unrealistic.

 The approach of pushing all your design work before you start writing your code is called *Big Design Up Front*, or *BDUF*. BDUF is often contrasted with the Agile, or iterative, development methodologies that have become more popular over the last 10–20 years. Since we find iterative approaches to be more effective, we've described the design process over the next couple of sections in an iterative manner.

In the previous chapter you saw an introduction to TDD—test-driven development— so by now you should be familiar with the fact that it's a good idea to start writing our project with a test class, `TwootrTest`. So let's start with a test that our user can log in: `shouldBeAbleToAuthenticateUser()`. In this test a user will log in and be correctly authenticated. A skeleton for this method can be seen in Example 6-1.

Example 6-1. Skeleton for shouldBeAbleToAuthenticateUser()

```
@Test
public void shouldBeAbleToAuthenticateUser()
{
    // receive logon message for valid user

    // logon method returns new endpoint.

    // assert that endpoint is valid
}
```

In order to implement the test we need to create a `Twootr` class and have a way of modeling the login event. As a matter of convention in this module any method that corresponds to an event happening will have the prefix on. So, for example, we're going to create a method here called `onLogon`. But what is the signature of this method—what information does it need to take as parameters and what should it reply with?

We've already made the architectural decision to separate our UI communications layer with a port. So here we need to make a decision as to how to define the API. We need a way of emitting events to a user—for example, that another user who the user is following has twooted. We also need a way of receiving events from a given user. In Java we can just use a method call to represent the events. So whenever a UI adapter wants to publish an event to `Twootr`, it will call a method on some object owned by the core of the system. Whenever `Twootr` wants to publish an event, it will call a method on some object owned by the adapter.

But the goal of ports and adapters is that we decouple the core from a specific adapter implementation. This means we need some way of abstracting over different adapters—an interface. We could have chosen to use an abstract class at this point in time. It would have worked, but interfaces are more flexible because adapter classes can implement more than one interface. Also by using an interface we're discouraging our future selves from the devilish temptation to add some state into the API. Introducing state in an API is bad because different adapter implementations may want to represent their internal state in a different way, so putting state into the API could result in coupling.

We don't need to use an interface for the object where user events are published as there will only be a single implementation in the core—we can just use a regular class. You can see what our approach looks like visually in Figure 6-6. Of course we need a name, or indeed a pair of names, in order to represent this API for sending and receiving events. There are lots of choices here; in practice, anything that made it clear that these were APIs for sending and receiving events would do well.

We've gone with `SenderEndPoint` for the class that sends events to the core and `ReceiverEndPoint` for the interface that receives events from the core. We could in fact flip the sender and receiver designations around to work from the perspective of the user or the adapter. This ordering has the advantage that we're thinking core first, adapters second.

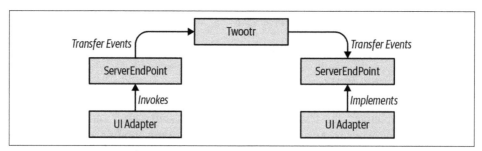

Figure 6-6. Events to code

Now that we know the route we're going down we can write the `shouldBeAbleToAuthenticateUser()` test. This just needs to test that when we log on to the system with a valid username that the user logs on. What does logging on mean here? Well, we want to return a valid `SenderEndPoint` object, as that is the object returned to the UI in order to represent the user who has just logged on. We then need to add a method to our `Twootr` class in order to represent the logon event happening and allow the test to compile. The signature of our implementation is shown in Example 6-2. Since TDD encourages us to do the minimal implementation work in order to get a test to pass and then evolve the implementation, we'll just instantiate the `SenderEndPoint` object and return it from our method.

Example 6-2. First onLogon signature

```
SenderEndPoint onLogon(String userId, ReceiverEndPoint receiver);
```

Now that we've got a nice green bar we need to write another test—`shouldNotAuthen ticateUnknownUser()`. This will ensure that we don't allow a user who we don't know about to log on to the system. When writing this test, an interesting issue crops up. How do we model the failure scenario here? We don't want to return a `SenderEnd Point` here, but we do need a way of indicating to our UI that the logon has failed. One approach would be to use exceptions, which we described in Chapter 3.

Exceptions could work here, but arguably it's a bit of an abuse of the concept. Failing to logon isn't really an exceptional scenario—it's a thing that happens all the time. People typo their username, they typo their passwords, and they can sometimes even go to the wrong website! An alternative, and common, approach would be to return the `SenderEndPoint` if the logon succeeds, and return `null` if it fails. This is a flawed approach for several reasons:

- If another developer uses the value without checking that it isn't `null`, they get a `NullPointerException`. These kinds of bugs are incredibly common mistakes for Java developers to make.
- There is no compile-time support in order to help avoid these kind of issues. They crop up at runtime.
- There is no way to tell from looking at the signature of a method whether it is deliberately returning a `null` value to model failure or whether there's just a bug in the code.

A better approach that can help here is to use the `Optional` data type. This was introduced in Java 8 and models values that may be present or absent. It's a generic type and can be thought of a box where a value may or may not lurk inside—a collection with only one or no values inside. Using `Optional` as a return type makes it explicit what happens when the method fails to return its value—it returns the empty `Optional`. We'll talk about how to create and use the `Optional` type throughout this chapter. So we now refactor our `onLogon` method to have the signature in Example 6-3.

Example 6-3. Second onLogon signature

```
Optional<SenderEndPoint> onLogon(String userId, ReceiverEndPoint receiver);
```

We also need to modify the shouldBeAbleToAuthenticateUser() test in order to
ensure that it checks that the Optional value is present. Our next test is shouldNotAu
thenticateUserWithWrongPassword() and is shown in Example 6-4. This test
ensures that the user who is logging in has the correct password for their logon to
work. That means our onLogon() method needs to not only store the names of our
users, but also their passwords in a Map.

Example 6-4. shouldNotAuthenticateUserWithWrongPassword

```
@Test
public void shouldNotAuthenticateUserWithWrongPassword()
{
    final Optional<SenderEndPoint> endPoint = twootr.onLogon(
        TestData.USER_ID, "bad password", receiverEndPoint);

    assertFalse(endPoint.isPresent());
}
```

A simple approach for storing the data in this case would have been to use a
Map<String, String>, where the key is the user ID and the value is the password. In
reality, though, the concept of a user is important to our domain. We've got stories
that refer to users and a lot of the system's functionality is related to users talking to
each other. It's time for a User domain class to be added to our implementation. Our
data structure will be modified to a Map<String, User>, where the key is the user's
ID and the value is the User object for the user in question.

A common criticism about TDD is that it discourages the design of software. That it
just leads you to write tests and you end up with an anaemic domain model and have
to just rewrite your implementation at some point. By an *anaemic domain model* we
mean a model where the domain objects don't have much business logic and it's all
scattered across different methods in a procedural style. That's certainly a fair critique
of the way that TDD can sometimes be practiced. Spotting the right point in time to
add a domain class or make some concept real in code is a subtle thing. If the concept
is something that your user stories are always referring to, though, you should really
have something in your problem domain representing it.

There are some clear anti-patterns that you can spot, however. For example, if you've
built different lookup structures with the same key, that you add to at the same time
but relate to different values, then you're missing a domain class. So if we track the set
of followers and the password for our user and we have two Map objects from the user

ID, one onto followers and one onto a password, then there's a concept in the problem domain missing. We actually introduced our User class here with only a single value that we cared about—the password—but an understanding of the problem domain tells us that users are important so we weren't being overly premature.

 From this point onward in the chapter we'll use the word "user" to represent the generic concept of a user, and the stylized User to represent the domain class. Similarly, we use Twootr to refer to the system as a whole, and Twootr to refer to the class that we're developing.

Passwords and Security

So far we've avoid talking about security at all. In fact, not talking about security concerns and hoping that they will just go away is the technology industries' favorite security strategy. Explaining how to write secure code isn't a primary, or even secondary, objective of this book; however, Twootr does use and store passwords for authentication so it's worth thinking a little about this topic.

The simplest approach to storing passwords is to treat them like any other String, known as storing them *plain text*. This is bad practice in general as it means anyone who has access to your database has access to the passwords of all your users. A malicious person or organization can, and in many cases has, used plain-text passwords in order to log in to your system and pretend to be the users. Additionally, many people use the same password for multiple different services. If you don't believe us, ask any of your elderly relatives!

In order to avoid anyone with access to your database just reading the passwords, you can apply a *cryptographic hash function* to the password. This is a function that takes some arbitrarily sized input string and converts it to some output, called a *digest*. Cryptographic hash functions are deterministic, so that if you want to hash the same input again you can get the same result. This is essential in order to be able to check the hashed password later. Another key property is that while it should be quick to go from input to digest, the reverse function should take so long or use so much memory that it is impractical for an attacker to reverse the digest.

The design of cryptographic hash functions is an active research topic on which governments and companies spend a lot of money. They are hard to implement correctly so you should never write your own—Twootr uses an established Java library called Bouncy Castle (*https://www.bouncycastle.org/*). This is open source and has undergone heavy peer review. Twootr uses the *Scrypt* hashing function, which is a modern algorithm specifically designed for storing passwords. Example 6-5 shows an example of the code.

Example 6-5. KeyGenerator

```
class KeyGenerator {
    private static final int SCRYPT_COST = 16384;
    private static final int SCRYPT_BLOCK_SIZE = 8;
    private static final int SCRYPT_PARALLELISM = 1;
    private static final int KEY_LENGTH = 20;

    private static final int SALT_LENGTH = 16;

    private static final SecureRandom secureRandom = new SecureRandom();

    static byte[] hash(final String password, final byte[] salt) {
        final byte[] passwordBytes = password.getBytes(UTF_16);
        return SCrypt.generate(
            passwordBytes,
            salt,
            SCRYPT_COST,
            SCRYPT_BLOCK_SIZE,
            SCRYPT_PARALLELISM,
            KEY_LENGTH);
    }

    static byte[] newSalt() {
        final byte[] salt = new byte[SALT_LENGTH];
        secureRandom.nextBytes(salt);
        return salt;
    }
}
```

A problem that many hashing schemes have is that even though they are very computationally expensive to compute, it may be feasible to compute a reversal of the hashing function through brute forcing all the keys up to a certain length or through a rainbow table (*https://oreil.ly/0y6Pc*). In order to guard against this possibility, we use a salt. *Salts* are extra randomly generated input that is added to a cryptographic hashing function. By adding some extra input to each password that the user wouldn't enter, but is randomly generated, we stop someone from being able to create a reverse lookup of the hashing function. They would need to know the hashing function and the salt.

Now we've mentioned a few basic security concepts here around the idea of storing passwords. In reality, keeping a system secure is an ongoing effort. Not only do you need to worry about the security of data at rest, but also data in flight. When someone connects to your server from a client, it needs to transmit the user's password over a network connection. If a malicious attacker intercepts this connection, they could take a copy of the password and use it to do the most dastardly thing possible in 140 characters!

In the case of Twootr, we receive a login message via WebSockets. This means that for our application to be secure the WebSocket connection needs to be secure against a man-in-the-middle attack. There are several ways to do this; the most common and simplest is to use *Transport Layer Security* (TLS), which is a cryptographic protocol that aims to provide privacy and data integrity to data sent out over its connection.

Organizations with a mature understanding of security build regular reviews and analysis into the design of their software. For example, they might periodically bring in outside consultants or an internal team to attempt to penetrate a system's security defenses by playing the role of a attacker.

Followers and Twoots

The next requirement that we need to address is following users. You can think about designing software in one of two different ways. One of those approaches, called *bottom-up*, starts with designing the core of the application—data storage models or relationships between core domain objects—works its way up to building the functionality of the system. A bottom-up way of looking at following between users would be to decide how to model the relationship between users that following entails. It's clearly a many-to-many relationship since each user can have many followers and a user can follow many other users. You would then proceed to layer on top of this data model the business functionality that is required to keep users happy.

The other approach is a *top-down* approach to software development. This starts with user requirements or stories and tries to develop the behavior or functionality needed to implement these stories, slowly driving down to the concerns of storage or data modeling. For example, we would start with the API for receiving an event to follow another user and then design whatever storage mechanism is needed for this behavior, slowly working from API to business logic to persistence.

It is hard to say that one approach is better in all circumstances and that the other should always be avoided; however, for the line-of-business type of applications that Java is very popular for writing our experience is that a top-down approach works best. This is because the temptation when you start with data modeling or designing the core domain of your software is that you can expend unncessary time on features that aren't necessary for your software to work. The downside of a top-down approach is that sometimes as you build out more requirements and stories your initial design can be unsatisfactory. This means that you need to take a vigilant and iterative approach to software design, where you constantly improve it over time.

In this chapter of the book we will show you a top-down approach. This means that we start with a test to prove out the functionality of following users, shown in Example 6-6. In this case our UI will be sending us a event to indicate that a user wants to follow another user, so our test will call the onFollow method of our end point with the unique ID of the user to follow as an argument. Of course, this method doesn't yet exist—so we need to declare it in the `Twootr` class in order to get the code to compile.

Modeling Errors

The test in Example 6-6 just covers the golden path of the following operation, so we need to ensure that the operation has succeeded.

Example 6-6. shouldFollowValidUser

```
@Test
public void shouldFollowValidUser()
{
    logon();

    final FollowStatus followStatus = endPoint.onFollow(TestData.OTHER_USER_ID);

    assertEquals(SUCCESS, followStatus);
}
```

For now we only have a success scenario, but there are other potential scenarios to think about. What if the user ID passed as an argument doesn't correspond to an actual user? What if the user is already following the user that they've asked to follow? We need a way of modeling the different results or statuses that this method can return. As with everything in life, there's a proliferation of different choices that we can make. Decisions, decisions, decisions…

One approach would be to throw an exception when the operation returns and return void when it succeeds. This could be a completely reasonable choice. It may not fall foul of our idea that exceptions should only be used for exceptional control flow, in the sense that a well-designed UI would avoid these scenarios cropping up under normal circumstances. Let's consider some alternatives, though, that treat the status like a value, rather than using exceptions at all.

One simple approach would be using a `boolean` value—`true` to indicate success and `false` to indicate failure. That's a fair choice in situations where an operation can either succeed or fail, and it would only fail for a single reason. The problem with the `boolean` approach in situations that have multiple failure scenarios is that you don't know *why* it failed.

Alternatively, we could use simple `int` constant values to represent each of the different failure scenarios, but as discussed in Chapter 3 when introducing the concept of exceptions, this is an error prone, type unsafe, and poor readability + maintainability approach. There is an alternative here for statuses that is type safe and offers better documentation: *enum* types. An `enum` is a list of predefined constant alternatives that constitutes a valid type. So anywhere that you can use an `interface` or a `class` you can use an `enum`.

But enums are better than `int`-based status codes in several ways. If a method returns you an `int` you don't necessarily know what values the `int` could contain. It's possible to add javadoc to describe what values it can take, and it's possible to define constants (static final fields), but these are really just lipstick on a pig. Enums can only contain the list of values that are defined by the `enum` declaration. Enums in Java can also have instance fields and methods defined on them in order to add useful functionality, though we won't be using that feature in this case. You can see the declaration of our follower status in Example 6-7.

Example 6-7. FollowStatus

```
public enum FollowStatus {
    SUCCESS,
    INVALID_USER,
    ALREADY_FOLLOWING
}
```

Since TDD drives us to write the simplest implementation to get a test passing, then `onFollow` method at this point should simply return the `SUCCESS` value.

We've got a couple of other different scenarios to think about for our `following()` operation. Example 6-8 shows the test that drives our thinking around duplicate users. In order to implement it we need to add a set of user IDs to our `User` class to represent the set of users that this user is following and ensure that the addition of another user isn't a duplicate. This is really easy with the Java collections API. There's already a `Set` interface that defines unique elements, and the `add` method will return `false` if the element that you're trying to add is already a member of the `Set`.

Example 6-8. shouldNotDuplicateFollowValidUser

```
@Test
public void shouldNotDuplicateFollowValidUser()
{
    logon();

    endPoint.onFollow(TestData.OTHER_USER_ID);

    final FollowStatus followStatus = endPoint.onFollow(TestData.OTHER_USER_ID);
    assertEquals(ALREADY_FOLLOWING, followStatus);
}
```

The test `shouldNotFollowInValidUser()` asserts that if the user isn't valid, then the result status will indicate that. It follows a similar format to `shouldNotDuplicateFollowValidUser()`.

Twooting

Now we've laid the foundations let's get to the exciting bit of the product—twooting! Our user story described how any user could send a twoot and that any followers who were logged in at that moment in time should immediately see the twoot. Now realistically we can't see that users will see the twoot immediately. Perhaps they're logged into their computer but getting a coffee, staring at another social network or, God forbid, doing some work.

By now you're probably familiar with the overall approach. We want to write a test for a scenario where a user who has logged on receives a twoot from another user who sends the twoot—`shouldReceiveTwootsFromFollowedUser()`. In addition to logging on and following, this test requires a couple of other concepts. First, we need to model the sending of a twoot, and thus add an `onSendTwoot()` method to the `Sender EndPoint`. This has parameters for the `id` of the twoot, so that we can refer back to it later, and also its content.

Second, we need a way of notifying a follower that a user has twooted—something that we can check has happened in our test. We earlier introduced the `ReceiverEnd Point` as a way of publishing messages out to users, and now is the time to start using it. We'll add an `onTwoot` method resulting in Example 6-9.

Example 6-9. ReceiverEndPoint

```
public interface ReceiverEndPoint {
    void onTwoot(Twoot twoot);
}
```

Whatever our UI adapter is will have to send a message to the UI to tell it that a twoot has happened. But the question is how do write a test that checks that this `onTwoot` method has been called?

Creating Mocks

This is where the concept of a *mock* object comes in handy. A mock object is a type of object that pretends to be another object. It has the same methods and public API as the object being mocked and looks to the Java type system as though it's another object, but it's not. Its purpose is to record any interactions, for example, method calls, and be able to *verify* that certain method calls happen. For example, here we want to be able to verify that the onTwoot() method of ReceiverEndPoint has been called.

 It might be confusing for people who have a computer science degree reading this book to hear the word "verify" being used in this way. The mathematics and formal methods communities tend to use it to mean situations where a property of a system has been proved for all inputs. Mocking uses the word totally differently. It just means checking that a method has been invoked with certain arguments. It's sometimes frustrating when different groups of people use the same word with overloaded meanings, but often we just need to be aware of the different contexts that terminology exists within.

Mock objects can be created in a number of ways. The first mock objects tended to be written by hand; we could in fact hand write a mock implementation of ReceiverEnd Point here, and Example 6-10 is an example of one. Whenever the onTwoot method is called we record its invocation by storing the Twoot parameter in a List, and we can verify that it has been called with certain arguments by making an assertion that the List contains the Twoot object.

Example 6-10. MockReceiverEndPoint

```
public class MockReceiverEndPoint implements ReceiverEndPoint
{
    private final List<Twoot> receivedTwoots = new ArrayList<>();

    @Override
    public void onTwoot(final Twoot twoot)
    {
        receivedTwoots.add(twoot);
    }

    public void verifyOnTwoot(final Twoot twoot)
    {
        assertThat(
            receivedTwoots,
            contains(twoot));
    }
}
```

In practice, writing mocks by hand can become tedious and error prone. What do good software engineers do to tedious and error-prone things? That's right—they automate them. There are a number of libraries that can help us by providing ways of creating mock objects for us. The library that we will use in this project is called *Mockito*, is freely available, open source, and commonly used. Most of the operations relating to *Mockito* can be invoked using static methods on the `Mockito` class, which we use here as static imports. In order to create the mock object you need to use the `mock` method, as shown in Example 6-11.

Example 6-11. mockReceiverEndPoint

```
private final ReceiverEndPoint receiverEndPoint = mock(ReceiverEndPoint.class);
```

Verifying with Mocks

The mock object that has been created here can be used wherever a normal `Receiver EndPoint` implementation is used. We can pass it as a parameter to the `onLogon()` method, for example, to wire up the UI adapter. Once the behavior under test—the *when* of the test—has happened our test needs to actually verify that the `onTwoot` method was invoked (the *then*). In order to do this we wrap the mock object using the `Mockito.verify()` method. This is a generic method that returns an object of the same type that it is passed; we simply call the method in question with the arguments that we expect in order to describe the expected interaction with the mock object, as shown in Example 6-12.

Example 6-12. verifyReceiverEndPoint

```
verify(receiverEndPoint).onTwoot(aTwootObject);
```

Something you may have noticed in the last section is the introduction of the `Twoot` class that we used in the signature of the `onTwoot` method. This is a value object that will be used to wrap up the values and represent a `Twoot`. Since this will be sent to the UI adapter it should just consist of fields of simple values, rather than exposing too much from the core domain. For example, in order to represent the sender of the twoot it contains the `id` of the sender rather than a reference to their `User` object. The `Twoot` also contains a `content` `String` and the `id` of the `Twoot` object itself.

In this system `Twoot` objects are immutable. As mentioned previously, this style reduces the scope for bugs. This is especially important in something like a value object that is being passed to a UI adapter. You really just want to let your UI adapter display the `Twoot`, not to alter the state of another user's `Twoot`. It's also worth noting that we continue to follow domain language here in naming the class `Twoot`.

Mocking Libraries

We're using Mockito in this book because it has nice syntax and fits our preferred way of writing mocks, but it's not the only Java mocking framework. Both Powermock and EasyMock are also popular.

Powermock can emulate Mockito syntax but it allows you to mock things that Mockito doesn't support; for example, final classes or static methods. There is some debate around whether it's ever a good idea to mock things like final classes—if you can't provide a different implementation of the class in production, then should you really really be doing so in tests? In general, Powermock usage isn't encouraged but there can occasionally be break-glass situations where it is useful.

EasyMock takes a different approach to writing mocks. This is a stylistic choice and may be preferred by some developers over others. The biggest conceptual difference is that EasyMock encourages strict mocking. Strict mocking is the idea that if you don't explicitly state that an invocation should occur, then it's an error to do so. This results in tests that are more specific about the behavior that a class performs, but that can sometimes become coupled to irrelevant interactions.

SenderEndPoint

Now these methods like `onFollow` and `onSendTwoot` are declared on the `SenderEnd` `Point` class. Each `SenderEndPoint` instance represents the end point from which a single user sends events into the core domain. Our design for `Twoot` keeps the `Sender` `EndPoint` simple—it just wraps up the main `Twootr` class and delegates to the methods passing in the `User` object for the user that it represents within the system. Example 6-13 shows the overall declaration of the class and an example of one method corresponding to one event—`onFollow`.

Example 6-13. SenderEndPoint

```
public class SenderEndPoint {
    private final User user;
    private final Twootr twootr;

    SenderEndPoint(final User user, final Twootr twootr) {
        Objects.requireNonNull(user, "user");
        Objects.requireNonNull(twootr, "twootr");

        this.user = user;
        this.twootr = twootr;
    }

    public FollowStatus onFollow(final String userIdToFollow) {
        Objects.requireNonNull(userIdToFollow, "userIdToFollow");

        return twootr.onFollow(user, userIdToFollow);
    }
```

You might have noticed the `java.util.Objects` class in Example 6-13. This is a utility class that ships with the JDK itself and offers convenience methods for `null` reference checking and implementation of `hashCode()` and `equals()` methods.

There are alternative designs that we could consider instead of introducing the `SenderEndPoint`. We could have received events relating to a user by just exposing the methods on the `Twootr` object directly, and expect to have any UI adapter call those methods directly. This is a subjective issue, like many parts of software development. Some people would consider creating the `SenderEndPoint` as adding unnecessary complexity.

The biggest motivation here is that, as mentioned earlier, we don't want to expose the `User` core domain object to a UI adapter—only talking to them in terms of simple events. It would have been possible to take a user ID as a parameter to all the `Twootr` event methods, but then the first step for every event would have been looking up the `User` object from the ID, whereas here we already have it in the context of the `SenderEndPoint`. That design would have removed the concept of the `SenderEndPoint`, but added more work and complexity in exchange.

In order to actually send the `Twoot` we need to evolve our core domain a little bit. The `User` object needs to have a set of followers added to it, who can be notified of the `Twoot` when it arrives. You can see code for our `onSendTwoot` method as it is implemented at this stage in the design in Example 6-14. This finds the users the who are logged on and tells them to receive the twoot. If you're not familiar with the `filter` and `forEach` methods or the `::` or `->` syntax, don't worry—these will be covered in "Functional Programming" on page 151.

Example 6-14. onSendTwoot

```
void onSendTwoot(final String id, final User user, final String content)
{
    final String userId = user.getId();
    final Twoot twoot = new Twoot(id, userId, content);
    user.followers()
        .filter(User::isLoggedOn)
        .forEach(follower -> follower.receiveTwoot(twoot));
}
```

The `User` object also needs to implement the `receiveTwoot()` method. How does a `User` receive a twoot? Well, it should notify the UI for the user that there's a twoot ready to be displayed by emitting an event, which entails calling `receiverEndPoint.onTwoot(twoot)`. This is the method call that we've verified the invocation of using mocking code, and calling it here makes the test pass.

You can see the final iteration of our test in Example 6-15, and this is the code that you can see if you download the example project from GitHub. You might notice it looks a bit different than what we've so far described. First, as the tests for receiving twoots have been written, a few operations have been refactored out into common methods. An example of this is logon(), which logs our first user onto the system—part of the given section of many tests. Second, the test also creates a Position object and passes it to the Twoot, and also verifies the interaction with a twootRepository. What the heck is a repository? Both of these are concepts that we've not needed so far, but are part of the evolution of the design of the system and will be explained in the next two sections.

Example 6-15. shouldReceiveTwootsFromFollowedUser

```
@Test
public void shouldReceiveTwootsFromFollowedUser()
{
    final String id = "1";

    logon();

    endPoint.onFollow(TestData.OTHER_USER_ID);

    final SenderEndPoint otherEndPoint = otherLogon();
    otherEndPoint.onSendTwoot(id, TWOOT);

    verify(twootRepository).add(id, TestData.OTHER_USER_ID, TWOOT);
    verify(receiverEndPoint).onTwoot(new Twoot(id, TestData.OTHER_USER_ID,
TWOOT, new Position(0)));
}
```

Positions

You will learn about Position objects very soon, but before presenting their definition we should meet their motivation. The next the requirement that we need to get working is that when a user logs in they should see all the twoots from their followers since they last logged in. This entails needing to be able to perform some kind of replay of the different twoots, and know what twoots haven't been seen when a user logs on. Example 6-16 shows a test of that functionality.

Example 6-16. shouldReceiveReplayOfTwootsAfterLogoff

```
@Test
public void shouldReceiveReplayOfTwootsAfterLogoff()
{
    final String id = "1";

    userFollowsOtherUser();

    final SenderEndPoint otherEndPoint = otherLogon();
    otherEndPoint.onSendTwoot(id, TWOOT);

    logon();

    verify(receiverEndPoint).onTwoot(twootAt(id, POSITION_1));
}
```

In order to implement this functionality, our system needs to know what twoots were sent while a user was logged off. There are lots of different ways that we could think about designing this feature. Different approaches may have different trade-offs in terms of implementation complexity, correctness, and performance/scalability. Since we're just starting out building Twootr and not expecting many users to begin with, focusing on scalability issues isn't our goal here:

- We could track the time of every twoot and the time that a user logs off and search for twoots between those times.

- We could think of twoots as a contiguous stream where each twoot has a position within the stream and record the position when a user logs off.

- We could use positions and record the position of the last seen twoot.

When considering the different designs we would lean away from ordering messages by time. It's the kind of decision that feels like a good idea. Let's suppose we store the time unit in terms of milliseconds—what happens if we receive two twoots within the same time interval? We wouldn't know the order between those twoots. What if a twoot is received on the same millisecond that a user logs off?

Recording the times at which users log off is another problematic event as well. It might be OK if a user will only ever log off by explicitly clicking a button. In practice, however, that's only one of several ways in which they can stop using our UI. Perhaps they'll close the web browser without explicitly logging off, or perhaps their web browser will crash. What happens if they connect from two web browsers and then log off from one of them? What happens if their mobile phone runs out of battery or closes the app?

We decided the safest approach to knowing from where to replay the twoots was to assign positions to twoots and then store the position up to which each user has seen. In order to define positions we introduce a small value object called Position, which is shown in Example 6-17. This class also has a constant value for the initial position where streams will be before the stream starts. Since all of our position values will be positive, we could use any negative integer for the initial position: -1 is chosen here.

Example 6-17. Position

```java
public class Position {
    /**
     * Position before any tweets have been seen
     */
    public static final Position INITIAL_POSITION = new Position(-1);

    private final int value;

    public Position(final int value) {
        this.value = value;
    }

    public int getValue() {
        return value;
    }

    @Override
    public String toString() {
        return "Position{" +
            "value=" + value +
            '}';
    }

    @Override
    public boolean equals(final Object o) {
        if (this == o) return true;
        if (o == null || getClass() != o.getClass()) return false;

        final Position position = (Position) o;

        return value == position.value;
    }

    @Override
    public int hashCode() {
        return value;
    }

    public Position next() {
        return new Position(value + 1);
```

```
        }
}
```

This class looks a little bit complex, doesn't it? At this point in your programming you may ask yourself: Why do I have these `equals()` and `hashCode()` methods defined on it, rather than just let Java handle them for me? What is a *value object*? Why am I asking so many questions? Don't worry, we have just introduced a new topic and will answer your questions soon. It is often very convenient to introduce small objects that represent values that are compounds of fields or give a relevant domain name to some numeric value. Our `Position` class is one example; another one might be the `Point` class that you see in Example 6-18.

Example 6-18. Point

```
class Point {
    private final int x;
    private final int y;

    Point(final int x, final int y) {
        this.x = x;
        this.y = y;
    }

    int getX() {
        return x;
    }

    int getY() {
        return y;
    }
```

A `Point` has an x coordinate and a y coordinate, while a `Position` has just a value. We've defined the fields on the class and the getters for those fields.

The equals and hashcode Methods

If we want to compare two objects defined like this with the same value, then we find that they aren't equal when we want them to be. Example 6-19 shows an example of this; by default, the `equals()` and `hashCode()` methods that you inherit from `java.lang.Object` are defined to use a concept of reference equality. This means that if you have two different objects located in different places in your computer's memory, then they aren't equal—even if all the field values are equal. This can lead to a lot of subtle bugs in your program.

Example 6-19. Point objects aren't equal when they should be

```
final Point p1 = new Point(1, 2);
final Point p2 = new Point(1, 2);
System.out.println(p1 == p2); // prints false
```

It's often helpful to think in terms of two different types of objects—*reference objects* and *value objects*—based upon what their notion of equality is. In Java we can override the `equals()` method in order to define our own implementation that uses the fields deemed relevant to value equality. An example implementation is shown in Example 6-20 for the `Point` class. We check that the object that we're being given is the same type as this object, and then check each of the fields are equal.

Example 6-20. Point equality definition

```
@Override
public boolean equals(final Object o) {
    if (this == o) return true;
    if (o == null || getClass() != o.getClass()) return false;

    final Point point = (Point) o;

    if (x != point.x) return false;
    return y == point.y;
}

@Override
public int hashCode() {
    int result = x;
    result = 31 * result + y;
    return result;
}
```

```
final Point p1 = new Point(1, 2);
final Point p2 = new Point(1, 2);
System.out.println(p1.equals(p2)); // prints true
```

The Contract Between equals and hashCode

In Example 6-20 we not only override the `equals()` method, but also the `hashCode()` method. This is due to the Java *equals/hashcode contract*. This states that if we have two objects that are equal according to their `equals()` method, they also have to have the same `hashCode()` result. A number of core Java APIs make use of the `hashCode()` method—most notably collection implementations like `HashMap` and `HashSet`. They rely on this contract holding true, and you will find that they don't behave as you would expect if it doesn't. So how do you correctly implement the `hashCode()`?

Good hashcode implementations not only follow the contract, but they also produce hashcode values that are evenly spread throughout the integers. This helps improve the efficiency of HashMap and HashSet implementations. In order to achieve both of those goals, the following is a simple series of rules that if you follow will result in a good hashCode() implementation:

1. Create a result variable and assign it a prime number.

2. Take each field that is used by the equals() method and compute an int value to represent the hashcode of the field.

3. Combine the hashcode from the field with the existing result by multiplying the previous result by a prime number; for example, result = 41 * result + hash codeOfField;

In order to calculate the hashcode for each field, you need to differentiate based upon the type of the field in question:

- If the field is a primitive value, use the hashCode() method provided on its companion class. For example, if it's a double then use Double.hashCode().

- If it's a nonnull object, just call its hashCode() method or use 0 otherwise. This can be abbreviated with the java.lang.Objects.hashCode() method.

- If it's an array, you need to combine the hashCode() values of each of its elements using the same rules as we've described here. The java.util.Arrays.hash Code() methods can be used to do this for you.

In most cases you won't need to actually write the equals() and hashCode() methods yourself. Modern Java IDEs will generate them for you. It's still helpful to understand the principles and reasons behind the code they generate, though. It's especially important to be able to review a pair of equals() and hashCode() methods that you see in code and know whether they are well or poorly implemented.

 We've talked in this section a little bit about value objects, but a future version of Java is scheduled to include *inline classes*. These are being prototyped in Project Valhalla (*https://oreil.ly/muvlT*). The idea behind inline classes is to provide a very efficient way to implement data structures that look like values. You will still be able to code against them like you can a normal class, but they will generate correct hashCode() and equals() methods, use up less memory, and for many use cases be faster to program with.

When implementing this feature we need to associate a `Position` with every `Twoot`, so we add a field to the `Twoot` class. We also need to record each user's last seen `Position`, so we add a `lastSeenPosition` to a `User`. When a `User` receives a `Twoot` they update their position, and when a `User` logs on they emit the twoots that the user hasn't seen. So no new events need to be added to either the `SenderEndPoint` or the `ReceiverEndPoint`. Replaying twoots also requires that we store the `Twoot` objects somewhere—initially, we just use a JDK `List`. Now our users don't have to be logged on to the system all the time in order to enjoy Twootr, which is awesome.

Takeaways

- You learned about bigger-picture architectural ideas like communication styles.
- You developed the ability to decouple domain logic from library and framework choices.
- You drove the development of code in this chapter with tests going outside-in.
- You applied object-oriented domain modeling skills to a larger project.

Iterating on You

If you want to extend and solidify the knowledge from this section you could try one of these activities:

- Try the word wrap Kata (*https://oreil.ly/vH2Q5*).
- Without reading the next chapter write down a list of things that need to be implemented in order for Twootr to be complete.

Completing the Challenge

We had a followup meeting with your client Joe and talked about the great progress that was made with the project. A lot of the core domain requirements have been covered and we've described how the system could be designed. Of course Twootr isn't complete at this point. You've not heard about how you wire the application up together so that the different components can talk to each other. You've also not been exposed to our approach to persist the state of twoots into some kind of storage system that won't disappear when Twootr is rebooted.

Joe is really excited by both the progress made and he's really looking forward to seeing the finished Twootr implementation. The final chapter will complete the design of Twootr and cover the remaining topics.

CHAPTER 7

Extending Twootr

The Challenge

Previously, on Twootr, Joe had wanted a modern online communication system to be implemented. The previous chapter presented a potential design for Twootr and the implementation of the core business domain was described, including driving out that design through tests. You learned about some of the design and data modeling decisions involved and how to break down the initial problem and structure your solution. That didn't cover the whole of the Twootr project, so it's up to this chapter to complete the narrative.

The Goal

This chapter extends and completes the progress made in the previous chapter by helping you understand about the following topics:

- Avoiding coupling with the Dependency Inversion Principle and Dependency Injection
- Persistence with the Repository pattern and the Query Object pattern.
- A brief introduction to functional programming that will show you how you can make use of the ideas from this in a Java-specific context and a real application.

Recap

Since we're continuing the Twootr project from the previous chapter, it's probably worth recapping the key concepts in our design at this point. If you're continuing from the previous chapter in a marathon reading session, then we're glad you're enjoying the book, but feel free to skip this section:

- Twootr is the parent class that instantiates the business logic and orchestrates the system.

- A Twoot is a single instance of a message broadcast by a user in our system.

- A ReceiverEndPoint is an interface that is implemented by a UI adapter and pushes Twoot objects out to the UI.

- The SenderEndPoint has methods that correspond to events being sent into the system from a user.

- Password management and hashing are performed by the KeyGenerator class.

Persistence and the Repository Pattern

So we've now got a system that can support much of the core twooting operations. Unfortunately, if we restart the Java process in any way all the twoots and user information is lost. We need a way of persisting the information that we're storing in order to survive a restart. Earlier in the discussion of software architecture we talked about ports and adapters and how we would like to keep the core of our application agnostic of the storage backend. There's, in fact, a commonly used pattern that helps us do this: the *Repository* pattern.

The Repository pattern defines an interface between the domain logic and storage backend. In addition to allowing us to use a different storage backend over time as our application evolves, this approach offers several advantages:

- Centralizing logic for mapping data from our storage backend to the domain model.

- Enables unit testing of core business logic without having to spin up a database. This can speed up the execution of tests.

- Improves maintainability and readability by keeping each class single responsibility.

You can think of a repository as a being like a collection of objects, but instead of just storing the objects in memory, the repository persists them somewhere. When evolving the design of our application we drove the design of the repositories through tests; however, to save time here we will just describe the final implementation. Since a repository is a collection of objects we need two of them in Twootr: one to store User objects and one for Twoot objects. Most repositories have a series of common operations that are implemented:

add()
> Stores a new instance of the object into the repository.

get()
> Looks up a single object based on an identifier.

delete()
> Deletes an instance from the persistence backend.

update()
> Ensures that the values saved for this object are equal to the instance fields.

Some people use the acronym CRUD to describe these kind of operations. This stands for Create, Read, Update, and Delete. We've used add and get instead of create and read as the naming is more inline with common Java usage, for example, in the collections framework.

Designing the Repositories

In our case we've designed things top-down and driven the development of the repositories from tests. The implication of this is that not all the operations are defined on both repositories. The UserRepository, shown in Example 7-1, doesn't have an operation to delete a User. That's because there's no requirement that has actually driven an operation to delete a user. We asked our customer, Joe, about this and he said "once you Twoot, you can't stop!"

When working on your own, you might be tempted to add functionality just to have the "normal" operations in the repository, but we would strongly caution against going down that route. Unused code, or *dead code* as it's often known, is a liability. In some sense all code is a liability, but if the code is actually doing something useful then it has a benefit to your system, while if it unused it's merely a liability. As your requirements evolve you need to refactor and improve your codebase and the more unused code that you have lying around, the more difficult this task is.

There's a guiding principle here that we've been alluding to throughout the chapter, but not mentioned until now: *YAGNI*. This stands for *You ain't gonna need it*. This doesn't mean don't introduce abstractions and different concepts like repositories. It just means don't write code that you think you're going to need in the future—only write it when you actually need it.

Example 7-1. UserRepository

```
public interface UserRepository extends AutoCloseable {
    boolean add(User user);

    Optional<User> get(String userId);

    void update(User user);

    void clear();

    FollowStatus follow(User follower, User userToFollow);
}
```

There are also differences between the design of our two repositories due to the nature of the objects that they are storing. Our Twoot objects are immutable, so the TwootRepository shown in Example 7-2 doesn't need to implement an update() operation.

Example 7-2. TwootRepository

```
public interface TwootRepository {
    Twoot add(String id, String userId, String content);

    Optional<Twoot> get(String id);

    void delete(Twoot twoot);

    void query(TwootQuery twootQuery, Consumer<Twoot> callback);

    void clear();
}
```

Normally the add() method in a repository simply takes the object in question and persists it to the database. In the case of the TwootRepository, we have taken a different approach. This method takes some specific parameters and actually creates the object in question. The motivation behind this approach was that the data source would be the one to assign the next Position object to the Twoot. We're delegating the responsibility of ensuring a unique and ordered object to the data layer that will have the appropriate tool for creating such a sequence.

Another alternative might have been to take a Twoot object that doesn't have a posi tion assigned to it and then have the position field set when it is added. Now one of the key goals of an object's constructor should be to ensure that all the internal state is completely initialized, ideally checked with final fields. By not assigning the position at object creation time we would have created an object that wasn't completely instantiated, breaking one of our principles around creating objects.

Some implementations of the Repository pattern introduce a generic interface—for example, something like Example 7-3. In our case this wouldn't be appropriate as the `TwootRepository` doesn't have an `update()` method and the `UserRepository` doesn't have a `delete()` method. If you want to write code that abstracts over different repositories, then this might be useful. Trying to avoid forcing different implementations into the same interface for the sake of it is a key part of designing a good abstraction.

Example 7-3. AbstractRepository

```
public interface AbstractRepository<T>
{
    void add(T value);

    Optional<T> get(String id);

    void update(T value);

    void delete(T value);
}
```

Query Objects

Another key distinction between different repositories is how they support querying. In the case of Twootr our `UserRepository` doesn't need any querying capability, but when it comes to `Twoot` objects we need to be able to look up the twoots to replay when a user logs on. What is the best way to implement this functionality?

Well, there are several different choices that we could make here. The simplest is that we could simply try our repository like a pure `Java Collection` and have a way of iterating over the different `Twoot` objects. The logic to query/filter could then be written in normal Java code. This is lovely, but potentially quite slow as it requires us to retrieve all the rows from our data store into our Java application in order to do the querying, when in reality we may only want a few of them. Often data store backends such as SQL databases have highly optimized and efficient implementations of how to query and sort data, and it's best to leave the querying to them.

Having decided that the repository implementation needs to have the responsibility for querying the data store we need to decide how best to expose this through the `TwootRepository` interface. One choice would have been to add a method that is tied to our business logic that performs the querying operation. For example, we could have written something like the `twootsForLogon()` method from Example 7-4 that takes the user object and looks up twoots associated with it. The downside of this is that we've now coupled the specific business logic functionality to our repository implementation—something that the introduction of our repository abstraction was designed to avoid. This will make it harder for us to evolve our implementation in line with requirements as we'll have to modify the repository as well as the core domain logic and also breaches the Single Responsibility Principle.

Example 7-4. twootsForLogon

```
List<Twoot> twootsForLogon(User user);
```

What we want to design is something that enables us to harness the power of a data store's querying capability without tying the business logic to the data store in question. We could add a specific method to query the repository for a given business criteria, as shown by Example 7-5. This approach is much better than the first two, but can still be refined a little bit. The problem with hardcoding each query to a given method is that as your application evolves over time and adds more querying functionality, we add more and more methods to the Repository interface, bloating it and making it harder to understand.

Example 7-5. twootsFromUsersAfterPosition

```
List<Twoot> twootsFromUsersAfterPosition(Set<String> inUsers, Position lastSeenPosi
tion);
```

This brings us to the next querying iteration, shown in Example 7-6. Here we've abstracted out the criteria that we query our `TwootRepository` on into its own object. Now we can add additional properties to this criteria to query on without having the number of query methods be a combinatorial explosion of different properties to query about. The definition of our `TwootQuery` object is shown in Example 7-7.

Example 7-6. query

```
List<Twoot> query(TwootQuery query);
```

Example 7-7. TwootQuery

```
public class TwootQuery {
    private Set<String> inUsers;
    private Position lastSeenPosition;

    public Set<String> getInUsers() {
        return inUsers;
    }

    public Position getLastSeenPosition() {
        return lastSeenPosition;
    }
```

```
public TwootQuery inUsers(final Set<String> inUsers) {
    this.inUsers = inUsers;

    return this;
}

public TwootQuery inUsers(String... inUsers) {
    return inUsers(new HashSet<>(Arrays.asList(inUsers)));
}

public TwootQuery lastSeenPosition(final Position lastSeenPosition) {
    this.lastSeenPosition = lastSeenPosition;

    return this;
}

public boolean hasUsers() {
    return inUsers != null && !inUsers.isEmpty();
}
}
```

This isn't the final design approach taken for querying the twoots, though. By return-ing a List of objects it means that we need to load into memory all the Twoot objects that are going to be returned in one go. This isn't a terribly good idea when this List may grow to be very large. We may not want to query all of the objects in one go either. That's the case here—we want to push each of the Twoot objects out to our UI without needing to have them all in memory at one point in time. Some repository implementations create an object to model the set of results returned. These objects let you page or iterate through the values.

In this case we're going to do something simpler: just take a Consumer<Twoot> call-back. That's a function that the caller is going to pass in that takes a single argument —a Twoot—and returns void. We can implement this interface using either a lambda expression or a method reference. You can see our final approach in Example 7-8.

Example 7-8. query

```
void query(TwootQuery twootQuery, Consumer<Twoot> callback);
```

See Example 7-9 to see how you would use this query method. This is how our onLogon() method calls the query. It takes the user who has logged on, and uses the set of users that this user is following as the user part of the query. It then uses the last seen position for that part of the query. The callback that receives the results of this query is user::receiveTwoot, a method reference to the function that we described earlier that publishes the Twoot object to the UI ReceiverEndPoint.

Example 7-9. An example of using the query method

```
twootRepository.query(
    new TwootQuery()
        .inUsers(user.getFollowing())
        .lastSeenPosition(user.getLastSeenPosition()),
    user::receiveTwoot);
```

That's it—that's our repository interface designed and usable in the core of the application logic.

There is another feature that some repository implementations use that we haven't described here, and that's the *Unit of Work* pattern. We don't use the Unit of Work pattern in Twootr, but it's often used in conjunction with the Repository pattern so its worth mentioning it here. A common thing for line-of-business applications to do is to have a single operation that performs many interactions with the data store. For example, you might be transferring money between two bank accounts and want to remove money from one back account and add it to the other bank account in the same operation. You don't want either of these operations to succeed without the other one succeeding—you don't want to put money into the creditor's account when there isn't enough money in the debtor's account. You also don't want to reduce the debtor's balance without ensuring that you can put money into the creditor account.

Databases often implement transactions and ACID compliance in order to enable people to perform these kinds of operations. A transaction is essentially a group of different database operations that are logically performed as a single, atomic operation. A Unit of Work is a design pattern that helps you perform database transactions. Essentially, each operation that you perform on your repository gets registered with a unit of work object. Your unit of work object can then delegate to one of more repositories, wrapping these operations in a transaction.

One thing we haven't talked about so far is how we actually implement the repository interfaces that we've designed. As with everything else in software development, there are often different routes we can go down. The Java ecosystem contains many Object-Relational Mappers (ORMs) that try to automate the task of this implementation for you. The most popular ORM is Hibernate (*http://hibernate.org/*). ORMs tend to be a simple approach that can automate some of the work for you; however, they often end up producing sub-optimal database querying code and can sometimes introduce more complexity than they help remove.

In the example project we provide two implementations of each of the repositories. One of them is a very simple in-memory implementation suitable for testing that won't persist the data over restarts. The other approach uses plain SQL and the JDBC API. We won't go into much detail about the implementation as most of it doesn't illustrate any particularly interesting Java programming ideas; however, in

"Functional Programming" on page 151 we will talk about how we use some ideas from functional programming in the implementation.

Functional Programming

Functional programming is a style of computer programming that treats methods as operating like mathematical functions. This means that it avoids mutable state and changing data. You can program in this style in any language, but some programming languages offer features to help make it easier and better—we call those *functional programming languages*. Java isn't a functional programming language, but in version 8, 20 years after it was first released, it started to add a number of features that helped make functional programming in Java a reality. Those features include lambda expressions, the Streams and Collectors API, and the Optional class. In this section we'll talk a little bit about how those functional programming features can be used and how we use them in Twootr.

There are limits to the level of abstractions that library writers could use in Java before Java 8. A good example of this was the lack of efficient parallel operations over large collections of data. Java from 8 onward allows you to write complex collection-processing algorithms, and simply by changing a single method call you can efficiently execute this code on multicore CPUs. In order to enable writing of these kinds of bulk data parallel libraries, however, Java needed a new language change: lambda expressions.

Of course there's a cost, in that you must learn to write and read lambda-enabled code, but it's a good trade-off. It's easier for programmers to learn a small amount of new syntax and a few new idioms than to have to handwrite a large quantity of complex thread-safe code. Good libraries and frameworks have significantly reduced the cost and time associated with developing enterprise business applications, and any barrier to developing easy-to-use and efficient libraries should be removed.

Abstraction is a concept that is familiar to anyone who does object-oriented programming. The difference is that object-oriented programming is mostly about abstracting over data, while functional programming is mostly about abstracting over behavior. The real world has both of these things, and so do our programs, so we can and should learn from both influences.

There are other benefits to this new abstraction as well. For many of us who aren't writing performance-critical code all the time, these are more important wins. You can write easier-to-read code—code that spends time expressing the intent of its business logic rather than the mechanics of how it's achieved. Easier-to-read code is also easier to maintain, more reliable, and less error-prone than code that is more difficult to read.

Lambda Expressions

We will define a lambda expression as a concise way of describing an anonymous function. We appreciate that's quite a lot to take in at once, so we're going to explain what lambda expressions are by working through an example of some existing Java code. Let's start by taking a interface used to represent a callback in our codebase: `ReceiverEndPoint`, shown in Example 7-10.

Example 7-10. ReceiverEndPoint

```
public interface ReceiverEndPoint {
    void onTwoot(Twoot twoot);
}
```

In this example, we're creating a new object that provides an implementation of the `ReceiverEndPoint` interface. This interface has a single method, `onTwoot`, which is called by the Twootr object when it is sending a `Twoot` object to the UI adapter. The class listed in Example 7-11 provides an implementation of this method. In this case to keep things simple we're just printing it out on the command line rather than sending a serialized version to an actual UI.

Example 7-11. Implementing ReceiverEndPoint with a class

```
public class PrintingEndPoint implements ReceiverEndPoint {
    @Override
    public void onTwoot(final Twoot twoot) {
        System.out.println(twoot.getSenderId() + ": " + twoot.getContent());
    }
}
```

This is actually an example of behavior parameterization—we're parameterizing over the different behaviors to send a message to the UI.

There are seven lines of boilerplate code required in order to call the single line of actual behavior here. Anonymous inner classes were designed to make it easier for Java programmers to represent and pass around behaviors. You can see an example in Example 7-12, which reduces the boilerplate a bit but they still don't make it easy enough if you want to make passing behavior around really easy.

Example 7-12. Implementing ReceiverEndPoint with an anonymous class

```
final ReceiverEndPoint anonymousClass = new ReceiverEndPoint() {
    @Override
    public void onTwoot(final Twoot twoot) {
        System.out.println(twoot.getSenderId() + ": " + twoot.getContent());
    }
};
```

Boilerplate isn't the only issue, though: this code is fairly hard to read because it obscures the programmer's intent. We don't want to pass in an object; what we really want to do is pass in some behavior. In Java 8 or later, we would write this code example as a lambda expression, as shown in Example 7-13.

Example 7-13. Implementing ReceiverEndPoint with a lambda expression

```
final ReceiverEndPoint lambda =
    twoot -> System.out.println(twoot.getSenderId() + ": " + twoot.getCon
tent());
```

Instead of passing in an object that implements an interface, we're passing in a block of code—a function without a name. twoot is the name of a parameter, the same parameter as in the anonymous inner class example. -> separates the parameter from the body of the lambda expression, which is just some code that is run when the twoot gets published.

Another difference between this example and the anonymous inner class is how we declare the variable event. Previously, we needed to explicitly provide its type: Twoot twoot. In this example, we haven't provided the type at all, yet this example still compiles. What is happening under the hood is that javac is inferring the type of the variable event from it's context—here, from the signature of onTwoot. What this means is that you don't need to explicitly write out the type when it's obvious.

 Although lambda method parameters require less boilerplate code than was needed previously, they are still statically typed. For the sake of readability and familiarity, you have the option to include the type declarations, and sometimes the compiler just can't work it out!

Method References

A common idiom you may have noticed is the creation of a lambda expression that calls a method on its parameter. If we want a lambda expression that gets the content of a Twoot, we would write something like Example 7-14.

Example 7-14. Get the content of a twoot

```
twoot -> twoot.getContent()
```

This is such a common idiom that there's actually an abbreviated syntax for this that lets you reuse an existing method, called a method reference. If we were to write the previous lambda expression using a method reference, it would look like Example 7-15.

Example 7-15. A method reference

```
Twoot::getContent
```

The standard form is `Classname::methodName`. Remember that even though it's a method, you don't need to use brackets because you're not actually calling the method. You're providing the equivalent of a lambda expression that can be called in order to call the method. You can use method references in the same places as lambda expressions.

You can also call constructors using the same abbreviated syntax. If you were to use a lambda expression to create a `SenderEndPoint`, you might write Example 7-16.

Example 7-16. Lambda to create a new SenderEndPoint

```
(user, twootr) -> new SenderEndPoint(user, twootr)
```

You can also write this using method references, as shown in Example 7-17.

Example 7-17. Method reference to create a new SenderEndPoint

```
SenderEndPoint::new
```

This code is not only shorter, but also a lot easier to read. `SenderEndPoint::new` immediately tells you that you're creating a new `SenderEndPoint` without your having to scan the whole line of code. Another thing to notice here is that method references automatically support multiple parameters, as long as you have the right functional interface.

When we were first exploring the Java 8 changes, a friend of ours said that method references "feel like cheating." What he meant was that, having looked at how we can use lambda expressions to pass code around as if it were data, it felt like cheating to be able to reference a method directly.

In fact, method references are really making the concept of first-class functions explicit. This is the idea that we can pass behavior around and treat it like another value. For example, we can compose functions together.

Execute Around

The *Execute Around* pattern is a common functional design pattern. You may encounter a situation where you have common initialization and cleanup code that you always want to do, but parameterize different business logic that runs within the initialization and cleanup code. An example of the general pattern is shown in Figure 7-1. There are a number of example situations in which you can use execute around, for example:

Files
> Open a file before you use it, and close it when you've finished using the file. You may also want to log an exception when something goes wrong. The parameterized code can read from or write to the file.

Locks
> Acquire a lock before your critical section, release the lock after your critical section. The parameterized code is the critical section.

Database connections
> Open a connection to a database upon initialization, close it when finished. This is often even more useful if you pool your database connections as it also allows your open logic to also retrieve the connection from your pool.

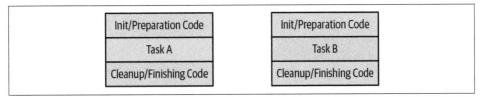

Figure 7-1. Execute Around pattern

Because the initialization and cleanup logic is being used in many places, it is possible to get into a situation where this logic is duplicated. This means that if you want to modify this common initialization or cleanup code, then you will have to modify multiple different parts of your application. It also exposes the risk that these different code snippets could become inconsistent, introducing potential bugs into your application.

The Execute Around pattern solves this problem by extracting a common method that defines both the initialization and cleanup code. This method takes a parameter containing the behavior that differs between use cases of the same overall pattern. The parameter will use an interface to enable it to be implemented by different blocks of code, usually using lambda expressions.

Example 7-18 shows a concrete example of an `extract` method. This is used within Twootr in order to run SQL statements against the database. It creates a prepared statement object for a given SQL statement and and then runs our `extractor` behavior on the statement. The `extractor` is just a callback that extracts a result, i.e., reads some data from the database, using the `PreparedStatement`.

Example 7-18. Use of the Execute Around pattern in the extract method

```
<R> R extract(final String sql, final Extractor<R> extractor) {
    try (var stmt = conn.prepareStatement(sql, Statement.RETURN_GENER
ATED_KEYS)) {
        stmt.clearParameters();
        return extractor.run(stmt);
    } catch (SQLException e) {
        throw new IllegalStateException(e);
    }
}
```

Streams

The most important functional programming features in Java are focused around the Collections API and *Streams*. Streams allow us to write collections-processing code at a higher level of abstraction than we would be able to do with loops. The `Stream` interface contains a series of functions that we'll explore throughout this chapter, each of which corresponds to a common operation that you might perform on a `Collection`.

map()

If you've got a function that converts a value of one type into another, `map()` lets you apply this function to a stream of values, producing another stream of the new values.

You may very well have been doing some kind of map operations for years already with for loops. In our `DatabaseTwootRepository` we've built up a tuple to be used in a query `String` containing all the `id` values of the different users whom a user is following. Each `id` value is a quoted `String` and the whole tuple is surrounded by brackets. For example, if they followed users with IDs `"richardwarburto"` and `"raoulUK"` we would produce a tuple `String` of `"(richardwarburto,raoulOK)"`. In order to generate this tuple you would use a mapping pattern, transforming each `id` into `"id"` and then adding them into a `List`. The `String.join()` method can then be used to join them with commas between. Example 7-19 is code written in this style.

Example 7-19. Building a user tuple with a for loop

```
private String usersTupleLoop(final Set<String> following) {
    List<String> quotedIds = new ArrayList<>();
    for (String id : following) {
        quotedIds.add("'" + id + "'");
```

```
        }
        return '(' + String.join(",", quotedIds) + ')';
    }
```

map() is one of the most commonly used Stream operations. Example 7-20 is the same example of building up the user tuple but using map(). It also takes advantage of the joining() collector, which allows us to join the elements in the Stream together into a String.

Example 7-20. Building a user tuple using map

```
    private String usersTuple(final Set<String> following) {
        return following
            .stream()
            .map(id -> "'" + id + "'")
            .collect(Collectors.joining(",", "(", ")"));
    }
```

The lambda expression passed into map() both takes a String as its only argument and returns a String. It isn't necessary for both the argument and the result to be the same type, but the lambda expression passed in must be an instance of Function. This is a generic functional interface with only one argument.

forEach()

The forEach() operation is useful when you want to perform a side effect for each value in the Stream. For example, suppose you want to print out the name of a user or save each transaction in your stream to a database. forEach() takes a single argument —a Consumer callback executed that gets invoked with every element in the stream as an argument.

filter()

Any time you're looping over some data and checking each element with an if statement, you might want to think about using the Stream.filter() method.

For example, the InMemoryTwootRepository needs to query the different Twoot objects in order to find twoots that meet its TwootQuery. Specifically, that the position is after the last seen position and that user is being followed. An example of this being written in for loop style is shown in Example 7-21.

Example 7-21. Looping over twoots and using an if statement

```
    public void queryLoop(final TwootQuery twootQuery, final Consumer<Twoot> call
back) {
        if (!twootQuery.hasUsers()) {
```

```
        return;
    }

    var lastSeenPosition = twootQuery.getLastSeenPosition();
    var inUsers = twootQuery.getInUsers();

    for (Twoot twoot : twoots) {
        if (inUsers.contains(twoot.getSenderId()) &&
            twoot.isAfter(lastSeenPosition)) {
            callback.accept(twoot);
        }
    }
}
```

You have probably written some code that looks like this: it's called the `filter` pattern. The central idea of filter is to retain some elements of the `Stream`, while throwing others out. Example 7-22 shows how you would write the same code in a functional style.

Example 7-22. Functional style

```
@Override
public void query(final TwootQuery twootQuery, final Consumer<Twoot> callback) {
    if (!twootQuery.hasUsers()) {
        return;
    }

    var lastSeenPosition = twootQuery.getLastSeenPosition();
    var inUsers = twootQuery.getInUsers();

    twoots
        .stream()
        .filter(twoot -> inUsers.contains(twoot.getSenderId()))
        .filter(twoot -> twoot.isAfter(lastSeenPosition))
        .forEach(callback);
}
```

Much like `map()`, `filter()` is a method that takes just a single function as an argument—here we're using a lambda expression. This function does the same job that the expression in the if statement did earlier. Here, it returns `true` if the `String` starts with a digit. If you're refactoring legacy code, the presence of an if statement in the middle of a for loop is a pretty strong indicator that you really want to use filter. Because this function is doing the same job as the if statement, it must return either `true` or `false` for a given value. The `Stream` after the `filter` has the elements of the `Stream` beforehand, which evaluated to `true`.

reduce()

reduce is a pattern that will also be familiar to anyone who has used loops to operate on collections. It's the kind of code that you write when you want to collapse down an entire list of values into a single value—for example, finding the sum of all the values of different transactions. The general pattern that you would see with reduction when writing a loop is shown in Example 7-23. Use the reduce operation when you've got a collection of values and you want to generate a single result.

Example 7-23. The reduce pattern

```
Object accumulator = initialValue;
for (Object element : collection) {
 accumulator = combine(accumulator, element);
}
```

An accumulator gets pushed through the body of the loop, with the final value of the accumulator being the value that we were trying to compute. The accumulator starts with an initialValue and then gets combined together with each element of the list by calling the combine operation.

The things that differ between implementations of this pattern are the initialValue and the combining function. In the original example, we used the first element in the list as our initialValue, but it doesn't have to be. In order to find the shortest value in a list, our combine would return the shorter track of out of the current element and the accumulator. We'll now take a look at how this general pattern can be codified by an operation in the Streams API itself.

Let's demonstrate the reduce operation by adding a feature that combines together different twoots into one large twoot. The operation will have a list of Twoot objects, the sender of the Twoot, and its id provided as arguments. It will need to combine together the different content value and return the highest position of the twoots being combined. The overall code is demonstrated in Example 7-24.

We start with a new Twoot object created using the id, senderId with empty content and the lowest possible position—the INITIAL_POSITION. The reduce then folds together each element with an accumulator, combining the element to the accumulator at every step. When we reach the final Stream element, our accumulator has the sum of all the elements.

The lambda expression, known as a reducer, performs the combining and takes two arguments. acc is the accumulator and holds the previous twoots that have been combined. It is also passed in the current Twoot in the Stream. The reducer in our example creates a new Twoot, with the max of the two positions, the concatenation of their content, and the specified id and senderId.

Example 7-24. Implementing sum using reduce

```
    private final BinaryOperator<Position> maxPosition = maxBy(comparingInt(Posi
tion::getValue));

    Twoot combineTwootsBy(final List<Twoot> twoots, final String senderId, final
String newId) {
        return twoots
            .stream()
            .reduce(
                new Twoot(newId, senderId, "", INITIAL_POSITION),
                (acc, twoot) -> new Twoot(
                    newId,
                    senderId,
                    twoot.getContent() + acc.getContent(),
                    maxPosition.apply(acc.getPosition(), twoot.getPosition())));
    }
```

Of course these `Stream` operations aren't that interesting on their own. They become really powerful when you combine them together to form a pipeline. Example 7-25 shows some code from `Twootr.onSendTwoot()` where we send twoots to the followers of a user. The first step is to call the `followers()` method, which returns a `Stream<User>`. We then use the `filter` operation to find the users who are actually logged in who we want to send the twoot to. Then we use the `forEach` operation to produce the desired side effect: sending a twoot to a user and recording the result.

Example 7-25. Use of Stream within the onSendTwoot method

```
    user.followers()
        .filter(User::isLoggedOn)
        .forEach(follower ->
        {
            follower.receiveTwoot(twoot);
            userRepository.update(follower);
        });
```

Optional

`Optional` is a core Java library data type, introduced in Java 8, that is designed to provide a better alternative to null. There's quite a lot of hatred for the old null value. Even the man who invented the concept, Tony Hoare, described it as "my billion-dollar mistake" (*https://oreil.ly/OaXWj*). That's the trouble with being an influential computer scientist—you can make a billion-dollar mistake without even seeing the billion dollars yourself!

`null` is often used to represent the absence of a value, and this is the use case that `Optional` is replacing. The problem with using null in order to represent absence is the dreaded NullPointerException. If you refer to a variable that is null, your code blows up. The goal of Optional is twofold. First, it encourages the coder to make appropriate checks as to whether a variable is absent in order to avoid bugs. Second, it documents values that are expected to be absent in a class's API. This makes it easier to see where the bodies are buried.

Let's take a look at the API for Optional in order to get a feel for how to use it. If you want to create an Optional instance from a value, there is a factory method called of(). The Optional is now a container for this value, which can be pulled out with get, as shown in Example 7-26.

Example 7-26. Creating an Optional from a value

```
Optional<String> a = Optional.of("a");

assertEquals("a", a.get());
```

Because an Optional may also represent an absent value, there's also a factory method called empty(), and you can convert a nullable value into an Optional using the ofNullable() method. You can see both of these methods in Example 7-27, along with the use of the isPresent() method, which indicates whether the Optional is holding a value.

Example 7-27. Creating an empty Optional and checking whether it contains a value

```
Optional emptyOptional = Optional.empty();
Optional alsoEmpty = Optional.ofNullable(null);

assertFalse(emptyOptional.isPresent());

// a is defined above
assertTrue(a.isPresent());
```

One approach to using Optional is to guard any call to get() by checking isPresent()—this is needed because a call to get() can throw a NoSuchElementException. Unfortunately, this approach isn't a very good coding pattern for using Optional. If you use it this way, all you've really done is to replicate the existing patterns for using null—where you would check if a value isn't null as a guard.

A neater approach is to call the orElse() method, which provides an alternative value in case the Optional is empty. If creating an alternative value is computationally expensive, the orElseGet() method should be used. This allows you to pass in a Supplier function that is called only if the Optional is genuinely empty. Both of these methods are demonstrated in Example 7-28.

Example 7-28. Using orElse() and orElseGet()

```
assertEquals("b", emptyOptional.orElse("b"));
assertEquals("c", emptyOptional.orElseGet(() -> "c"));
```

Optional also has a series of methods defined that can be used like the Stream API; for example, filter(), map(), and ifPresent(). You can think of these methods applying to the Optional API similarly to the Stream API, but in this case your Stream can only contain 1 or 0 elements. So Optional.filter() will retain an element in the Optional if it meets the criteria and return an empty Optional if the Optional was previously empty or if the predicate fails to apply. Similarly, map() transforms the value inside the Optional, but if it's empty it doesn't apply the function at all. That's what makes these functions safer than using null—they only operate on the Optional if there's really something inside of it. ifPresent is the Optional dual of forEach—it applies a Consumer callback if there's a value there, but not otherwise.

You can see an extract of the code from the Twootr.onLogon() method in Example 7-29. This is an example of how we can put together these different operations to perform a more complex operation. We start off by looking up the User from their ID by calling UserRepository.get(), which returns an Optional. We then validate the user's password matchers using filter. We use ifPresent to notify the User of the twoots that they've missed. Finally, we map the User object into a new Sender EndPoint that is returned from the method.

Example 7-29. Use of Optional within the onLogon method

```
        var authenticatedUser = userRepository
            .get(userId)
            .filter(userOfSameId ->
            {
                var hashedPassword = KeyGenerator.hash(password, userOfSameId.get
Salt());
                return Arrays.equals(hashedPassword, userOfSameId.getPassword());
            });

        authenticatedUser.ifPresent(user ->
        {
            user.onLogon(receiverEndPoint);
```

```
        twootRepository.query(
            new TwootQuery()
                .inUsers(user.getFollowing())
                .lastSeenPosition(user.getLastSeenPosition()),
            user::receiveTwoot);
        userRepository.update(user);
    });

    return authenticatedUser.map(user -> new SenderEndPoint(user, this));
```

In this section we've really only scratched the surface of functional programming. If you are interested in learning about functional programming in greater depth, we recommend *Java 8 In Action* (*https://oreil.ly/wGImJ*) and *Java 8 Lambdas* (*https://oreil.ly/hDrfH*).

User Interface

Throughout this chapter we've avoided talking too much about the user interface to this system, because we're focused on the design of the core problem domain. That said, it's worth delving a little into what the example project delivers as part of its UI just in order to understand how the event modeling fits together. In our example project we ship a single-page website that uses JavaScript to implement its dynamic functionality. In order to keep things simple and not delve too much into the myriad framework wars, we've just used jquery to update the raw HTML page, but kept a simple separation of concerns in the code.

When you browse to the Twootr web page it connects back to the host using Web-Sockets. These were one of the event communication choices discussed back in "From Events to Design" on page 117. All the code for communicating with it lies in the web_adapter subpackage of chapter_06. The WebSocketEndPoint class implements the ReceiverEndPoint and also invokes any needed methods on the Sender EndPoint. For example, when the ReceiverEndPoint receives and parses a message to follow another user it invokes the SenderEndPoint.onFollow(), passing the username through. The returned enum—FollowStatus then gets converted into a wire format response and written down the WebSocket connection.

All communication between the JavaScript frontend and the server is done using the *JavaScript Object Notation* (JSON) standard (*http://www.json.org/*). JSON was chosen as it's very easy for a JavaScript UI to deserialize or serialize.

Within the WebSocketEndPoint we need to map to and from JSON within Java code. There are many libraries that can be used for this purpose, here we've chosen the Jackson library (*https://github.com/FasterXML/jackson*), which is commonly used and well maintained. JSON is often used in applications that take a request/response approach rather than an event-driven approach as well. In our case we manually extract the fields from the JSON object to keep things simple, but its also possible to use a higher-level JSON API, such as a binding API.

Dependency Inversion and Dependency Injection

We've talked a lot about decoupling patterns in this chapter. Our overall application uses the Ports and Adapters pattern and the Repository pattern to decouple business logic away from implementation details. There is in fact a large, unifying principle that we can think of when we see these patterns—*Dependency Inversion*. The Dependency Inversion Principle is the final of our five SOLID patterns that we've talked about in this book, and like the others was introduced by Robert Martin. It states that:

- High-level modules should not depend upon low-level modules. Both should depend upon abstractions.

- Abstractions should not depend upon details. Details should depend upon abstractions.

The principle is called an inversion because in traditional imperative, structured programming it is often the case that high-level modules compose down to produce low-level modules. It's often a side effect of the top-down design that we talked about in this chapter. You split up a big problem into different subproblems, write a module to solve each of those subproblems, and then the main problem (the high-level module) depends on the subproblems (the low-level modules).

In the design of Twootr we've avoided this problem through the introduction of abstractions. We have a high-level entry point class, called Twootr, and it doesn't depend upon the low-level modules such as our DataUserRepository. It depends upon the abstraction—the UserRepository interface. We perform the same inversion at the UI port. Twootr doesn't depend upon the WebSocketEndPoint—it depends upon the ReceiverEndPoint. We program to the interface, not the implementation.

A related term is the concept of *Dependency Injection*, or *DI*. To understand what DI is and why we need it, let's undertake a thought experiment on our design. Our architecture has determined that the main Twootr class needs to depend upon the UserRepository and TwootRepository in order to store User and Twoot objects. We have defined fields inside Twootr to store instances of these objects, as shown in Example 7-30. The question is, how do we instantiate them?

Example 7-30. Dependencies within the Twootr class

```
public class Twootr
{
```

```
private final TwootRepository twootRepository;
private final UserRepository userRepository;
```

The first strategy that we could use for populating the fields is to try and call constructors using the new keyword, as shown in Example 7-31. Here we've hardcoded the use of the database-based repositories into the codebase. Now most of the code in the class still programs to the interface, so we could change the implementation here quite easily without having to replace all our code, but it's a bit of a hack. We have to always use the database repositories, which means our tests for the Twootr class depend upon the database and run more slowly.

Not only that, but if we want to ship different versions of Twootr to different customers—for example, an in-house Twootr for enterprise customers that uses SQL and a cloud-based version that uses a NoSQL backend—we would have to cut the builds from two different versions of the codebase. It's not enough to just define interfaces and separate implementation—we also have to have a way of wiring up the right implementation in a way that doesn't break our abstraction and decoupling approach.

Example 7-31. Hardcoding the field instantiation

```
public Twootr()
{
    this.userRepository = new DatabaseUserRepository();
    this.twootRepository = new DatabaseTwootRepository();
}

// How to start Twootr
Twootr twootr = new Twootr();
```

A commonly used design pattern for instantiating different dependencies is the Abstract Factory Design pattern. Example 7-32 demonstrates this pattern, where we have a factory method that we can use to create an instance of our interface using the getInstance() method. When we want to set up the right implementations to use, we can call a setInstance(). So, for example, we could use setInstance() in tests to create an in-memory implementation, in an on-premise installation to use a SQL database, or in our cloud environment to use a NoSQL database. We've decoupled the implementation from the interface and can call this wiring code wherever we want.

Example 7-32. Creating the instances with factories

```
public Twootr()
{
    this.userRepository = UserRepository.getInstance();
    this.twootRepository = TwootRepository.getInstance();
}
```

```
// How to start Twootr
UserRepository.setInstance(new DatabaseUserRepository());
TwootRepository.setInstance(new DatabaseTwootRepository());
Twootr twootr = new Twootr();
```

Unfortunately this factory method approach has its downsides as well. For a start, we've now created a big ball of shared mutable state. Any situation where we want to run a single JVM with different Twootr instances with different dependencies isn't possible. We've also coupled together lifetimes—perhaps we sometimes want to instantiate a new TwootRepository when we start Twootr, or perhaps we sometimes want to reuse an existing one. The factory method approach won't let us directly do this. It can also become rather complicated to have a factory for every dependency that we want to create in our application.

This is where Dependency Injection comes in. DI can be thought of as an example of the Hollywood Agent approach—don't call us, we'll call you. With DI instead of creating dependencies explicitly or using factories to create them, you simply take a parameter and whatever instantiates your object has the responsibiltiy for passing in the required dependencies. It might be a test class's setup method passing in a mock. It might be the main() method of your application passing in a SQL database implementation. An example of this in use with the Twootr class is shown in Example 7-33. Dependency Inversion is a strategy; Dependency Injection and the Repository pattern are tactics.

Example 7-33. Creating the instances using Dependency Injection

```
public Twootr(final UserRepository userRepository, final TwootRepository twootReposi
tory)
{
    this.userRepository = userRepository;
    this.twootRepository = twootRepository;
}

// How to start Twootr
Twootr twootr = new Twootr(new DatabaseUserRepository(), new DatabaseTwootReposi
tory());
```

Taking objects this way not only makes it easier to write tests for your objects, but it has the advantage of externalizing the creation of the objects themselves. This allows your application code or a framework to control when the UserRepository is created and what dependencies are wired into it. Many developers find it convenient to use DI frameworks, such as Spring and Guice, that offer many features on top of basic DI. For example, they define lifecycles for beans that standardize hooks to be called after the objects are instantiated or before they are destroyed if required. They can also offer scopes for objects, such as Singleton objects that are only instantiated once during the lifetime of a process or per-request objects. Furthermore, these DI frameworks often hook nicely into web development frameworks such as Dropwizard or Spring Boot and provide a productive out-of-the-box experience.

Packages and Build Systems

Java allows you to split your codebase into different packages. Throughout this book we've put the code for each chapter into its own package and Twootr is the first project where we've split out multiple subpackages within the project itself.

Here are the packages can you look at for the different components within the project:

- `com.iteratrlearning.shu_book.chapter_06` is the top-level package for the project.
- `com.iteratrlearning.shu_book.chapter_06.database` contains the adapter for SQL database persistence.
- `com.iteratrlearning.shu_book.chapter_06.in_memory` contains the adapter for in-memory persistence.
- `com.iteratrlearning.shu_book.chapter_06.web_adapter` contains the adapter for the WebSockets-based UI.

Splitting out large projects into different packages can be helpful to structure code and make it easier for developers to find. Just in the same way that classes group together related methods and state, packages group together related classes. Packages should follow similar coupling and cohesion rules to your classes. Put classes in the same package when they're likely to change at the same time and are related to the same structure. For example, in the Twootr project if we want to alter the SQL database persistence code we know we go to the `database` subpackage.

Packages also enable information hiding. We discussed the idea of having a package-scoped constructor method back in Example 4-3 in order to prevent objects from being instantiated outside of the package. We can also have package scoping for classes and methods. This prevents objects outside of the package from accessing the details of the class and helps us achieve loose coupling. For example, `WebSocketEndPoint` is package-scoped implementation of the `ReceiverEndPoint` interface that lives in the `web_adapter` package. No other code in the project should talk to this class directly—only through the `ReceiverEndPoint` interface that acts as the port.

Our approach of having a package per adapter in Twootr fits nicely with the hexagonal architectural pattern that we've used throughout this module. Not every application is hexagonal, however, and there are two common package structures that you may well encounter in other projects.

One very common approach to structuring packages is to structure them by layer—for example, grouping together all code that generates HTML views in a website into a views package, and all the code that relates to handling web requests into a controller package. Despite being popular, this can be a poor choice of structure as it results in poor coupling and cohesion. If you want to modify an existing web page to add an additional parameter and display a value based upon that parameter, you would end up touching the controller and the view packages, and probably several others as well.

An alternative way of structuring code is to group code by feature. So, for example, if you were writing an ecommerce site you might have a cart package for your shopping cart, a product package for code related to product listings, a payment package code related to taking card payments, etc. This can often be more cohesive. If you want to add support for receiving payment by Mastercard as well as Visa, then you would only need to modify the payment package.

In "Using Maven" on page 55 we talked about how to set up a basic build structure using the Maven build tool. In the project structure for this book we have one Maven project and the different chapters of the book are different Java packages within that one project. That's a nice and simple project structure that will work for a wide range of different software projects, but it's not the only one. Both Maven and Gradle offer project structures that build and output many build artifacts from a single top-level project.

This can make sense if you want to deploy different build artifacts. For example, suppose you've got a client/server project where you want to have a single build that builds both the client and the server, but the client and the server are different binaries running on different machines. It's best not to overthink or over-modularize build scripts, though.

They're something that you and your team will be running on your machines regularly and the highest priority is for them to be simple, fast, and easy to use. That's why we went down the route of having one single project for the entire book, rather than submodule per project.

Limitations and Simplifications

You've seen how we implement Twootr and learned about our design decisions along the way, but does that mean that the Twootr codebase that we've seen so far is the only or the best way to write it? Of course not! In fact, there are a number of limitations to our approach and simplifications that we've deliberately taken in order to make the codebase explainable in a single chapter.

For a start we've written Twootr as though it will be run on a single thread and completely ignored the issue of concurrency. In practice we may want to have multiple threads responding to and emitting events in our Twootr implementation. That way we can make use of modern multicore CPUs and serve a larger number customers on one box.

In a bigger-picture sense, we've also ignored any kind of failover that would allow our service to continue to run if the server that it was hosted on fell over. We've also ignored scalability. For example, requiring all our twoots have a single defined order is something that is easy and efficient to implement on a single server but would present a serious scalability/contention bottleneck. Similarly, seeing all the twoots when you log on would cause a bottleneck as well. What if you go on holiday for a week and when you log back on you get 20,000 twoots!

Addressing these issues in detail goes beyond the scope of this chapter. However, these are important topics if you wish to go further with Java, and we plan to address them in greater detail in future books in this series.

Takeaways

- You can now decouple data storage from business logic using the Repository pattern.
- You have seen implementations of two different types of repositories within this approach.
- You were introduced to the ideas of functional programming, including Java 8 Streams.
- You've seen how to structure a larger project with different packages.

Iterating on You

If you want to extend and solidify the knowledge from this section you could try one of the following activities.

Suppose that we had taken a pull model for Twootr. Instead of having messages continuously pushed out to a browser-based client over WebSockets, we had used HTTP to poll for the latest messages since a position.

- Brainstorm how our design would have changed. Try drawing a diagram of the different classes and how data would flow between them.
- Implement, using TDD, this alternative model for Twootr. You don't need to implement the HTTP parts, just the underlying classes following this model.

Completing the Challenge

We built the product and it worked. Unfortunately, Joe realized when he launched that someone called Jack had released a similar product, with a similar name, taking billions in VC funding and with hundreds of millions of users. Jack only got there first by 11 years; it was bad luck for Joe, really.

CHAPTER 8

Conclusion

If you've read this far, you've hopefully enjoyed the book. We enjoyed writing it as well. In this concluding chapter you'll learn about where to go next in your programming career. We'll offer some advice on how to evolve your skills and push yourself to the next level in your career as a developer.

Project-Based Structure

The project-based structure of the book was designed to help you understand software development concepts more easily. You were presented topics within software projects in order to understand the context of software engineering decisions. Context is critical in software engineering—decisions that may be right in one context aren't so applicable in another. Many developers overuse and abuse subclassing due to misunderstanding that it's a mechanism for code reuse. Hopefully we've discouraged that idea in your mind in Chapter 4.

But you can't simply hope to read a book and magically become an expert software developer. It takes practice, experience, and patience. This book is just here to help optimize and improve the process. That's why we've added an "Iterating on You" section to each chapter—they offer suggestions as to how you can take the material in this book further and improve your understanding.

Iterating on You

As a software developer you probably often approach projects in an iterative fashion. That's to say, slice off the highest priority week or two's worth of work items, implement them, and then use the feedback in order to decide on the next set of items. We've found that it's often worth evaluating the progress of your own skills in the same way.

Taking a regular retrospective on yourself can help you gain focus and direction should you need it. Agile software development often involves weekly retrospectives, but you don't personally need to do it so frequently. A quarterly or biannual retrospective can be very helpful. One topic we've found useful is to evaluate what skills would help your current or a future job. In order to ensure that these skills are progressed, it's helpful to set a goal for the next quarter. This could be something to learn or something to improve upon. It doesn't need to a big goal like learning a whole new programming language; it could be something simple like picking up a new testing framework or a couple of design patterns.

We've heard pushback from some developers when it comes to skills. A frequently asked question is "How can I be constantly expected to learn new technologies, practices, and principles?" It's not easy and everyone is busy. They trick is to not worry about trying to learn everything in the technology industry. That's a surefire route to madness! Finding key skills that will serve you over time and build upon your existing skillset is what helps you become an excellent developer. The key thing is to be always improving yourself and iterating on you.

Deliberate Practice

While this book has covered a lot of the key concepts and skills that are needed to be a good developer, it's important to practice them. Reading isn't enough on its own—practice helps you internalize these skills and apply them yourself. In your day job seeking out situations where different techniques are appropriate to apply will help. As every pattern described in the book has places where it works and places where it doesn't work, so it's also helpful to consider situations where a technique isn't helpful.

Often we think that natural talent and intellect are the most crucial factors to success, but a lot of research has established that practice and work are the real the key to success. Books such as *Talent is Overrated* by Geoff Colvin (Portfolio, 2008) and *Outliers: The Story of Success* by Malcolm Gladwell (Penguin, 2009) evaluate a number of key factors to being successful in your life, and the most effective of all is deliberate practice.

Deliberate practice is a form of practice that has purpose and is systematic. Deliberate practice has the goal of trying to improve performance and requires focus and attention. Often when people practice their skills to improve them, they just engage in repetition. Doing the same thing over and over again expecting to get better at it is not the most effective way of doing things.

One good example of this was when we were exploring and learning the Eclipse Collections library (*https://www.eclipse.org/collections/*). In order to understand and learn the library in a systematic way we stepped through the excellent set of code Katas that come with the library in question. To ensure that we were getting a really good understanding, we stepped through the Katas three times. Each time we started from scratch and compared my solution with the one that we had done previously, finding cleaner, better, and faster ways of doing them.

The thing is that repeating personal behaviors means that they are automatic. So if you pick up bad habits during your career, you can end up teaching them to yourself through practicing on the job. Experience reinforces habit. Deliberate practice is the way to break out of that cycle. Deliberate practice may involve practicing new approaches from books systematically. It may involve taking a small problem that you've solved before and solving it repeatedly with different approaches. It may involve going on training courses that have exercises that have been designed to practice. No matter which route you go down, deliberate practice is the key to honing your skills over time and going beyond what this book covers.

Next Steps and Additional Resources

OK, so hopefully you're convinced that this book isn't the end of the road in terms of learning, but what should you look at next?

Getting involved in open source is a great way to learn more about software and expand your horizons. Many of the most popular Java open source projects, like JUnit and Spring are hosted on GitHub (*https://github.com/*). Some projects can be more welcoming than others but often open source maintainers are overworked and in need of help on their projects. You could take a look at the bug tracker and see if there's anything you can work.

Formal training courses and online learning are another practical and popular way of improving your skills. Online training courses are increasingly popular and both Pluralsight (*http://pluralsight.com/*) and the O'Reilly Learning Platform (*http://safaribook sonline.com/*) have a great selection of Java training courses.

Another fantastic source of information for developers are blogs and Twitter. Both Richard (*http://twitter.com/richardwarburto*) and Raoul (*https://twitter.com/raouluk*) are on Twitter and often post links on software development. The Programming Reddit (*http://reddit.com/r/programming*) often acts as a strong link aggregator, as does Hacker News (*http://news.ycombinator.com/*). Finally, the training company that the book authors run (Iteratr Learning) also provides a series of free articles (*http://iteratr learning.com/articles*) for anyone to read.

Thank you for reading this book. We appreciate your thoughts and feedback and wish you the best in your journey as a Java developer.

Index

Symbols

<> (diamond) operator, 100
@FunctionalInterface annotation, 34
@Test annotation, 25
    expected =+ attribute, 86
@throws Javadoc syntax, 51

A

abstract classes, 122
abstract factory design pattern, 165
abstraction, 151
    details and, 164
    in functional programming, benefits of, 151
accumulators, 159
Action interface, 91
    mocking and verifying interaction with
        Action object, 95
    refactoring so perform method can use
        Facts object as argument, 98
actions, 90, 107
    action using facts, 99
    action using facts and local variable type
        inference, 101
    adding to business rules engine, 96
    testing an Action with facts, 97
adapters, 119
    decoupling core from specific adapter
        implementation, 122
add method in repositories, 145
    TwootRepository (example), 146
aggregations
    avoiding returning primitive values from,
        40
    implementing with Streams API, 40

Agile, or iterative, development methodologies,
    121
    iterating on you, 171
anaemic domain model, 124
Android push notifications, 118
anti-cohesion, 38
anti-patterns, 9
    code duplication, 10
    exposing private state through getters/
        setters, 82
    God class, 9
    in test naming, 80
    indicating need for a domain class, 124
APIs
    designing a Fluent API, 106-111
    explicit vs. implicit API, 38-41
    for sending and receiving events, 122
assertAttributeEquals method, 83
assertion statements, 26
    Assert.fail method, 26
    assertAttributeEquals method, 83
    assertEquals method, 26, 85
    assertThat method, 85
    assertTrue method, 84
    summary of, 27
    using for testing, 26
AssertionError, 84
attributes
    and hierarchical Documents, 68
    assertAttributeEquals method, 83
    for importers in document management
        system, 70
    searching on attributes of a Document, 70
authentication, 120

About the Authors

Dr. Raoul-Gabriel Urma is the CEO and founder of Cambridge Spark, a leader in transformational data science and AI training, career development, and progression. He is author of several programming books, including the best seller *Modern Java in Action* (Manning). Raoul-Gabriel holds a PhD in Computer Science from Cambridge University as well as an MEng in Computer Science from Imperial College London and graduated with first-class honors, having won several prizes for technical innovation. His research interests lie in the area of programming languages, compilers, source code analysis, machine learning, and education. He was nominated an Oracle Java Champion in 2017. He is also an experienced international speaker, having delivered talks covering Java, Python, Artificial Intelligence, and Business. Raoul has advised and worked for several organizations on large-scale software engineering projects including at Google, Oracle, eBay, and Goldman Sachs.

Dr. Richard Warburton is the cofounder of Opsian.com and maintainer of the Artio FIX Engine. He's worked as a developer in different areas including developer tools, HFT, and network protocols. He has written the book *Java 8 Lambdas* for O'Reilly and helps developers learn via *http://iteratrlearning.com* and *http://www.pluralsight.com/author/richard-warburton*. Richard is an experienced conference speaker, having spoken at dozens of events and sat on conference committees for some of the biggest conferences in Europe and the USA. He holds a PhD in Computer Science from the University of Warwick.

Colophon

The animal on the cover of *Real-World Software Development* is a collared mangabey (*Cercocebus torquatus*), an Old World monkey found in a range along the west coast of Africa. The mangabey lives in forest habitat within both swamps and valleys. It spends most of its time in trees (climbing as high as 100 feet), but also scavenges for food on the ground, particularly during the dry season. It has a varied diet of fruit, seeds, nuts, plants, mushrooms, insects, and bird eggs.

The collared mangabey is so named for the white fur surrounding its head and neck, in contrast to the darker grey of its body. The monkey also has a striking chestnut-red patch on its head and white eyelids (which lend character to an already expressive face). The species weighs an average of 20-22 pounds and is 18-24 inches tall. Like many arboreal primates, the mangabey has a long flexible tail that is longer than its body—and the Latin name *Cercocebus* in fact means "tail monkey."

Mangabeys live in large groups of 10 to 35, made up of an alpha male and assorted females and juveniles. Adult males live alone until they can form or find a troop (the name for a group of mangabeys) to lead. Equipped with large amplifying throat-sacs, these animals are very vocal, with a large repertoire of shrieks, grunts, cackles, and other calls that serve to alert the troop to predators or warn away an intruder. Unfortunately, the amount of noise made by mangabeys also makes them easy targets for human hunters in search of bushmeat. They are listed as endangered.

Many of the animals on O'Reilly covers are endangered; all of them are important to the world.

The cover illustration is by Karen Montgomery, based on a black and white engraving from *Meyers Kleines Lexicon*. The cover fonts are Gilroy Semibold and Guardian Sans. The text font is Adobe Minion Pro; the heading font is Adobe Myriad Condensed; and the code font is Dalton Maag's Ubuntu Mono.

O'REILLY®

There's much more where this came from.

Experience books, videos, live online training courses, and more from O'Reilly and our 200+ partners—all in one place.

Learn more at oreilly.com/online-learning